THE ART OF MEMOIR

the ART OF MEMOIR

Mary Karr

HARPER

An Imprint of HarperCollins*Publishers*

HarperCollins books may be purchased for educational, business, or sales promotional use. For information, please e-mail the Special Markets Department at SPsales@harpercollins.com.

FIRST EDITION 809.9

Library of Congress Cataloging-in-Publication Data has been applied for.

ISBN: 978-0-06-222306-7

15 16 17 18 19 OV/RRD 10 9 8 7 6 5 4 3 2 1

To Sarah Harwel & Brooks Haxton
for decades of showing me how

Every one of us is shadowed by an illusory person: a false self. I wind my experiences around myself and cover myself with glory like bandages in order to make myself perceptible to myself and to the world, as if I were an invisible body that could only become visible when something visible covered its surface. But there is no substance under the things with which I am clothed, I am hollow, and my structure of pleasures and ambitions has no foundation. I am objectified in them. But they are all destined by their contingency to be destroyed. And when they are gone there will be nothing left but my own nakedness and emptiness and hollowness, to tell me I am my own mistake.

Thomas Merton, *Seeds of Contemplation*

So finally I would write one true sentence, and then go on from there. It was easy then because there was always one true sentence that I knew or had seen or had heard someone say. If I started to write elaborately, or like someone introducing or presenting something, I found that I could cut the scrollwork or ornament out and throw it away and start with the first true simple declarative sentence I had written.

Ernest Hemingway, *A Moveable Feast*

Life is a field of corn. Literature is the shot glass it distills down into.

Lorrie Moore

Contents

| CONTENTS |

Caveat Emptor

No one elected me the boss of memoir. I speak for no one but myself. Every writer worth her salt is sui generis. Memoirists' methods—with regard to handling actual events, memory, research, dealing with family and other subjects, legal whatnot, voice, etc.—differ from mine as widely as their lives do. Where I've learned from others, I add it. But this is no compendium of popular approaches to the form.

Also, there's a place in hell for writers who quote themselves and a few times, I am forced to recap adventures reported elsewhere. If I didn't have to pay out the wazoo to quote from better books than my own, I'd have way more Nabokov in here. An appendix at the back cites great memoirs. A concerted study of those will no doubt pay off for you as it did for me. Maybe the methods I use to parse books will help you fall in love with those masterpieces.

Special thanks to masters of various nonfiction forms I interviewed for this book: Philip Gourevitch, Kathryn Harrison, Michael Herr, Jon Krakauer, Larissa MacFarquhar, Jerry Stahl, Gary Shteyngart, Cheryl Strayed, Geoffrey Wolff. Over the decades, conversations with others have schooled me: Martin Amis, Maya Angelou, Fr. Edward Beck, Bill Buford, Robert Caro, Frank Conroy, Rodney Crowell, Mark Doty, Dave

Eggers, Lucy Grealy, Maxine Hong Kingston, Phil Jackson, Fr. James Martin, SJ, Peter Matthiessen, James McBride, Frank McCourt, Carolyn See, Lisa See, John Edgar Wideman, Tobias Wolff, Koren Zailckas. Dmitri Nabokov informed my thinking about his father's memoir.

Finally, much of what I say may well apply to writing novels or poems or love letters or bank applications or parole board pleas—in short, any kind of scribbling. But since it's memoir they've paid me for, I'll stick to it.

Preface | Welcome to My Chew Toy

Don't follow me, I'm lost,
the master said to the follower
who had a cocked pen and a yellow pad.

Stephen Dunn, "Visiting the Master"

This preface is a squeaky rubber chew toy I have pawed and gnawed at for years. Problem being, memoir as a genre has entered its heyday, with a massive surge in readership the past twenty years or so. But for centuries before now, it was an outsider's art—the province of weirdos and saints, prime ministers and film stars. As a grad student thirty years back, I heard it likened to inscribing the Lord's Prayer on a grain of rice. So I still feel some lingering obligation to defend it.

Partly what murders me about memoir—what I adore—is its democratic (some say ghetto-ass primitive), anybody-who's-lived-can-write-one aspect. You can count on a memoirist being passionate about the subject. Plus its structure remains dopily episodic. Novels have intricate plots, verse has musical forms, history and biography enjoy the sheen of objective truth. In memoir, one event follows another. Birth leads to puberty leads to sex. The books are held together by happenstance, theme, and (most powerfully) the sheer, convincing poetry of a single person trying to make sense of the past.

Changes in the novel have helped to jack up memoir's audience. As fiction grew more fabulist or dystopic or hyperintellectual under the sway of Joyce and Woolf and García Márquez and Pynchon acolytes, readers thirsty for reality began imbibing memoir.

Between 2005 and 2010, Philip Gourevitch closely observed the skyrocketing of nonfiction as literature at the editorial helm of that towering literary mag the *Paris Review*. (Gourevitch's classic on the Rwandan genocide, *We Wish to Inform You That Tomorrow We Will Be Killed with Our Families*, is also a masterpiece.) Here's an excerpt of his speech as he stepped down, likening rebukes against memoir as a lesser form to the critics who once mocked photography for lacking the originality of painting:

> The past fifty years has seen an explosion of exciting
> new work in memoir, reportage, and the literature
> of fact in all forms and lengths and styles. And yet,
> I am afraid, there is a kind of lingering snobbery
> in the literary world that wants to disqualify what
> is broadly called nonfiction from the category of
> "literature"—to suggest that somehow, it lacks in
> artistry, or imagination or invention by comparison to
> fiction. . . . But the nonfiction I published was every
> bit as good as fiction.

Youngsters may not recall the lengthy assaults against memoir from critics like William Gass[*] and Jonathan Yardley

---

[*] "The Art of Self: Autobiography in the Age of Narcissism," *Harper's*, May 1994, http://harpers.org/archive/1994/05/the-art-of-self/.

and James Wolcott. Their ultimately impotent campaigns put me in mind of how early novels were mocked for being mere "fancies," lacking the moral rigor of philosophy and sermons and the formal rigor of poetry.

So after fifty-plus years of reading every memoir I could track down and thirty teaching the best ones (plus getting paid to bang out three), I spent last year trying to cobble up what a physicist would call a Unified Field Theory or Theory of Everything about the form. I imagined a better me would have done this already. (A better me, says the nattering voice in my head, wouldn't eat Oreos by the sleeve.) This better me has an alphabetized bookshelf and a mind parceled out into Power-Point slides. She has a big fat overarching system.

In search of such a system, I found myself last winter shoving a wobbly-wheeled cart at Staples. Hours later, I lunged all snow-spackled into the house like a Labrador dragging home kill in her teeth. I got presentation easels (three), aluminum-framed slabs of corkboard (four), flip chart (one), and boo-coup color-coordinated index cards and sticky notes.

But by summer, the living room—now dubbed The War Room—resembled nothing so much as the headquarters of a serial killer task force, with cards tacked up and schematics and arrows and notes by color on the windowpanes. Index cards said stuff like: "Tell about Michael Herr and skinned man!" One quoted old Saint Augustine (probably a sex addict and arguably the father of memoir circa the fifth century—no, it's not Oprah): "Give me chastity, Lord, but not yet." I spent months watching the black cursor flicker, or with my nose in various books I wish I'd written. And I resisted the urge to slink off to hide under the bed like a dog with a bad haircut.

As with everything I've ever written, I start out paralyzed

by fear of failure. The tarantula ego—starving to be shored up by praise—tries to scare me away from saying simply whatever small, true thing is standing in line for me to say.

Ts'ok. That's why the Lord in infinite wisdom gave us delete keys.

Recently, a friend I teach with talked me down off the ledge about this project by reminding me that I've spent decades talking with joy to students about memoir. What I really bring to the classroom is having cherished the form as long and as hard as anybody. In 1965 I wrote, "When I grow up, I will write ½ poetry and ½ autobiography." And as a strange child reading the sagas of Helen Keller and Maya Angelou, I just felt less lonely. In some animistic way, I believed they were talking (as my toddler son once said of the infuriatingly saccharine Mr. Rogers) "only to me."

A first-person coming-of-age story, putatively true, never failed to give the child me hope that I could someday grow up and get out of the mess I was in—which was reading hours per day in a state of socially sanctioned disassociation to try and fence myself off from the chaos of my less-than-ideal household. If Angelou, born black in pre–civil rights Arkansas, and poor blind/deaf Keller each made it outta their own private hells to become that most exalted of creatures—a writer— maybe I could too. Every memoirist had lived to tell the tale, and that survival usually geezed me with hope as if with a hypodermic. A comparable-sounding novel just couldn't infuse me the same way.

However often fiction has served as a fig leaf for lived, remembered experience, the form doesn't promise veracity of event. As I turn a novel's pages, a first-person narrator may seduce me, but the fact that it's all made up and not actually outlived oddly keeps me from drawing courage outside the book's dream. The deep, mysterious sense of identification with a memoirist who's confessed her past just doesn't translate to a novelist I love, however deliciously written the work.

I'm embarrassed to confess this, because it sounds so naive—"identifying" with someone I've never met, a peddler of pages who profits from my buying her act. I sound like the guy at a strip club who thinks the dancers really fancy him.

I once heard Don DeLillo quip that a fiction writer starts with meaning and then manufactures events to represent it; a memoirist starts with events, then derives meaning from them. In this, memoir purports to grow more organically from lived experience. When I asked a class of undergrads what they liked about memoir, I heard them echo the no-doubt-naive sentiment that they drew hope from the mere fact of a writer living past a bad juncture to report on it. "It's a miracle he even survived!" was written on many papers. The telling has some magic power for them, as it does for me. "Tell it," the soldiers in Vietnam begged Michael Herr, and in *Dispatches*, he told it.

This confidence of mine in most memoirs' veracity is viewed as gullible, I know. Of course, there's artifice to the relationship between any writer and her reader. Memoir done right is an art, a made thing. It's not just raw reportage flung splat on the page. Most morally ominous: from the second you choose one event over another, you're shaping the past's meaning. Plus, memoir uses novelistic devices like cobbling together dialogue you failed to record at the time. To concoct a distinctive voice, you often have to do a poet's lapidary work. And the good ones reward study. You're making an experience for a reader, a show that conjures your past—inside and out—with enough lucidity that a reader gets way more than just the brief flash of titillation. You owe a long journey, and most of all, you owe all the truth you can wheedle out of yourself. So while it is a shaped experience, the best ones come from the soul of a human unit oddly compelled to root out the past's truth for his own deeply felt reasons.

In fact, every memoirist I know seems doomed to explore the past in an often-agonized death march down the pages. If you met them all at a cocktail party, they'd strike you as frank and upfront, more curious about the past than defensive about their own versions.

Think of that family meal we've all had when each person's colliding version of an event ricochets off every other. *You weren't even born when that happened.* At such a meal, I may defend my own account like a wolf her turf, but lying awake later, I'll often feel the creeping suspicion I'm wrong.

Unless you're a doubter and a worrier, a nail-biter, an apologizer, a *re*thinker, then memoir may not be your playpen. That's the quality I've found most consistently in those life-story writers I've met. Truth is not their *enemy*. It's the bannister they grab for when feeling around on the dark cellar stairs. It's the solution.

Wow, there it is, my long-lost theory, stolen obviously from the Delphic oracle with her pesky, near-impossible demand to "know thyself." A curious mind probing for truth may well set your scribbling ass free. A fierce urge to try reexperiencing your own mind and body and throbbing heart alive inside the most vivid stories from your past is step one. (No doubt if you weren't haunted by those stories, you wouldn't waste your time trying to write it.) Then you just have to tell it, right? The second-hardest part. I've inserted the words "the truth" to re-place the word "God" in the quote below from monk Thomas Merton's memoir *Seven-Storey Mountain*:

> The secret of my identity is hidden in the love and mercy of the truth. . . . The truth utters me like a word containing a partial thought to himself. A word will never be able to comprehend the voice that utters it.

With that idea in the air like rain mist, I usually enter one of my memoir classes like some kid coming off the beach with a roaring shell to press to everybody's ear. My big message is: Listen up. I'm a passionate, messy teacher. I give a rat's ass, and my sole job is to help students fall in love with what I al-ready worship, which means, I show you stuff I've read that I can't live without—*Black Boy* (aka *American Hunger*), *I Know Why the Caged Bird Sings, A Childhood: The Biography of a Place, Dispatches, The Woman Warrior, Stop-Time, The Kiss, Down and Out in Paris and London, Homage to Catalonia, The Color of Water, Good-Bye to All That, The Possessed: Adventures with Rus-sian Books and the People Who Read Them, Memories of a Catholic Girlhood, Wild, The Duke of Deception, This Boy's Life,* and *Speak, Memory*—then I'll lay out any wisdom about the form I've either gleaned from them or figured out on my own watch. For the prospective memoirist, I pepper in short lists and lessons.

That's what you'll get here—me running back and forth between books I've taught and my own dispatches from the muddy trenches, where I wrote three books that basically beat my Texas ass.

. . .

There's a photo of writer Harry Crews on my office door students often ask about because it looks so savagely unliterary. On an English Department hall lined with posters of prim Dickinson in white eyelet lace or that trying-to-be-sinister fop Baudelaire in black velvet, Crews strikes a muscleman pose. Wearing a jean jacket with the sleeves ripped out, he curls up his arm so the bicep's big as a ham hock. His face is pockmarked, grizzled, with a more-than-once smashed nose. Academia embraces virtually nothing blue collar, and Crews's image is a small assertion of my humble roots amid the stubbornly white-collar milieu of white tower academia (obvious emphasis on the *white*, which also predominates). Crews's meaty fist aims at his own chin as if he's about to knock himself out with an uppercut. Which I guess he was, as he kept on drinking Rebel whiskey way past when it did him any good. (Once after a binge, he found inside his elbow the still-bloody tattoo he had no recollection of getting—a hinge where his arm bent, as if he were machine, not flesh.)

In some ways, writing a memoir is knocking yourself out with your own fist, if it's done right. Sure, there's the pleasure of doing work guaranteed to engage you emotionally—who's indifferent to their own history? The form *always* has profound psychological consequence on its author. It can't not. What project can match it for that? Plus you get to hang out with folks no longer on this side of the grass. Places and times you may have for decades ached after wind up erecting themselves around you as you work.

But nobody I know who's written a great one described it as anything less than a major-league shit-eating contest. Any time you try to collapse the distance between your delusions about the past and what really happened, there's suffering involved. When I'm trying to edit or coach somebody through one, I usually wind up feeling like the mean sergeant played by Tom Berenger in *Platoon*. He's leaning over a screaming soldier whose guts are extruding, and in a husky whisper, Berenger says through gritted teeth, "Take the pain," till the guy shuts up and mechanically starts stuffing his guts back in.

No matter how self-aware you are, memoir wrenches at your insides precisely because it makes you battle with your very self—your neat analyses and tidy excuses. One not-really-a-joke saying in my family is, "The trouble started when you hit me back." Your small pieties and impenetrable, mostly unconscious poses invariably trip you up.

In terms of cathartic affect, memoir is like therapy, the difference being that in therapy, *you* pay *them*. The therapist is the mommy, and you're the baby. In memoir, you're the mommy, and the reader's the baby. And—hopefully—*they* pay *you*. ("No man but a blockhead ever wrote for any cause but money," Samuel Johnson said.)

So forget about holes in your memory or lawsuits or how those crazy suckers you share DNA with are going to spaz out once you tell about what Uncle Bubba did during naptime. (I'll talk later about how you can deal with all those worries.) You can do "research," i.e. postponing writing, till Jesus dons a nightie. But your memoir's real enemy is blinking back at you from the shaving glass when you floss at night—your ignorant ego and its myriad masks.

Crews's grossly overlooked *A Childhood: The Biography of a Place* magically pointed out to me my own lah-dee-dah poses. It's underrated—virtually unknown—except among the aficionados of the form. I used to worry it wasn't as good as I thought (particularly when Crews's fiction never wowed me) until I decided any aversion to it was a form of abject classism, which insists on marginalizing any working-class scribbler.

At the time I came across *A Childhood*, I was an academically uncredentialed former redneck Texan trying to pass myself off as a poet in hyperliterary Cambridge. Crews had lost time trying to hide his own cracker past, and then he'd written about that milieu in a book that would serve as my lodestar. How good it is, I can no longer gauge. But it helped to guide me out from my biggest psychological hidey-holes. Reading Crews, I found the courage to tell the stories I'd been amassing my whole life. I include so much of him here to underscore how mysterious a single influence can be if he shares a novice's foibles. Were I a tattoo-getting individual, I'd owe him some fleshly real estate.

I'd owe a lot of other people, too. I'd wind up like the state fair's illustrated woman, emblazoned with the inked-in faces of the best memoirists. Probably without Crews, I'd have eventually gotten around to my first book. But reading him, which I started doing circa 1980, gave me a shortcut—that sharp awareness of all the false selves I'd concocted for the page that kept me from speaking the truth with the stoppering power of duct tape over my mouth.

At least one purpose of this book is to lay out some lucky gliding spaces for a wannabe memoirist, to help her discover The Story, the one only she can tell; then to help said person craft a voice exactly suited to telling that tale in the truest, most beautiful way. By true, I mean without trying to pawn off fabricated events. By beautiful, I mean for the reader.

What's the test of beauty? Rereading. A memoir you return

to usually feels so intimate—believable, real—that you're lured back time and again. You miss its geography and atmosphere. Its characters are like old pals you pine after.

However many intellectual pleasures a book may offer up, it's usually your emotional connection to the memoir's narrator that hooks you in. And how does she do that? A good writer can conjure a landscape and its peoples to live inside you, and the best writers make you feel they've disclosed their soft underbellies. Seeing someone naked thrills us a little.

Maybe I can help prospective writers feel better about disrobing. My lessons and tips for anyone seeking to write a memoir are sprinkled in like pepper—"Why Not to Write a Memoir" or "Carnality" or "How to Choose a Detail." They're small and pithy enough that the general reader can pole-vault over those technical blips for students. In a late chapter on Michael Herr, there's an initial section for the general reader, and section two is a line-by-line analysis that a nonwriter might find tedious.

But the book's mostly shaped for the general reader, and while I hope it can help such a human hone an affection for memoir as a form, I really hope to prompt some reflection about the reader's own divided selves and ever-morphing past.

For everybody has a past, and every past spawns fierce and fiery emotions about what it means. Nobody can be autonomous in making choices today unless she grasps how she's being internally yanked around by stuff that came before. So this book's mainly for that person with an inner life big as Lake Superior and a passion for the watery element of memory. Maybe this book will give you scuba fins and a face mask and more oxygen for your travels.

THE ART OF MEMOIR

1 | The Past's Vigor

We look at the world once, in childhood.
The rest is memory.

Louise Glück, "Nostos"

At unexpected points in life, everyone gets waylaid by the colossal force of recollection. One minute you're a grown-ass woman, then a whiff of cumin conjures your dad's curry, and a whole door to the past blows open, ushering in uncanny detail. There are traumatic memories that rise up unbidden and dwarf you where you stand. But there are also memories you dig for: you start with a clear fix on a tiny instant, and pick at every knot until a thin thread comes undone that you can follow back through the mind's labyrinth to other places. We've all interrogated ourselves—*It couldn't have been Christmas because we had shorts on in the snapshot*. Such memories start by being figured out, but the useful ones eventually gain enough traction to haul you through the past.

Memory is a pinball in a machine—it messily ricochets around between image, idea, fragments of scenes, stories you've heard. Then the machine goes tilt and snaps off. But most of the time, we keep memories packed away. I sometimes liken that moment of sudden unpacking to circus clowns pouring out of a miniature car trunk—how did so much fit into such a small space?

You show up at your high school reunion shocked to find a middle-aged populace rather than the teens you passed in the hallways decades back. Then somebody mentions she sat behind you in Miss Pickett's seventh-grade English class, and somehow her prepubescent face blooms awake in you. Then you remember where your locker was that year, and that speech class came after English, and since speech was last period you walked home across the football field's fresh-mown grass, watching the boy you had a crush on in practice gear.

So a single image can split open the hard seed of the past, and soon memory pours forth from every direction, sprouting its vines and flowers up around you till the old garden's taken shape in all its fragrant glory. Almost unbelievable how much can rush forward to fill an absolute blankness.

On the first day of a memoir class, I often try to douse my students' flaming certainty about the unassailability of their memories. Usually I fake a fight with a colleague—prof or student—while a videographer whirs in back. Then the class is asked to record right after the event what happened.

For the caliber of grad students I face down, the exercise should be a slam-dunk. A year or so back almost eight hundred applied for six slots in poetry and six in fiction. They're all broke out in smarts, but in some oddball ways. Sure there are Ivy Leaguers, but in poetry we once turned down a Harvard grad for a gay ex-marine. In fiction, a Yale summa cum laude lost a seat to a former Barnum & Bailey clown.

Picture a seminar room with tables in a horseshoe and some

twenty grad students, mostly in black, each propping up a sty-rofoam cup of lukewarm liquid. I explain the videographer in back by saying a class transcript may help with a book on memoir I'm writing.

Following a script, I apologize for leaving my phone on but claim I have an administrative problem to work out half-way through our three-hour class. At planned intervals, my coconspirator, Chris sometimes, calls, putatively to ask—harangue?—me about swapping classrooms. The students hear me be jovial and accommodating, though I hustle him off the phone, saying let's talk at the break.

An hour before he's due, Chris steams in. A tall, fiftyish poet with a shaved head, he's tight-lipped his mouth into a line and is claiming that this is his seminar room. We need to clear out. Now.

We're playing against type. He's known as low-key and easygoing, and I as—how to say it?—noisy? Southern? He raises his voice. I suggest we step outside. He steps forward, I step back. He's tall, I'm short. I try to defuse the situation. He says for once I should do what everybody else does and coop-erate. He tells me to go fuck myself—or do I only remember it that way? Then he heaves a sheaf of papers into the air and stalks out. The students are agog. On the tape, they cut their eyes away from us to connect with each other.

Paralyzed silence. Am I okay? the codependent kid asks, Bambi-eyed. I explain the ruse, and the group's burst of laugh-ter is a collective awkwardness. One joker claims he's suing for trauma, since he flashed back to his parents fighting.

You'd guess that these bright, mostly young, fairly sensitive witnesses would nail the event down to the color of Chris's socks. And yet around the room, with each student reading from spiral notebook or legal pad the mistakes pop up like dandelion greens.

There are memory aces, of course. Maybe one, rarely two—of twenty to twenty-five per seminar—come with wizardly photographic recall. They get the facts spot on. They nail quotes verbatim and don't mess up physical details, or even intervals of time. (Getting time wrong is a common memory screw up, even for the young.) How often did he call? The wizards are dead certain it was three times, with ten- to twelve-minute gaps in between. And Chris's pants were khaki, his shirt denim, not vice versa; he wore not loafers but black Nikes double-knotted with two holes unthreaded. Marvels, these observers.

Reviewing student blunders in these classes, I correct details on the board, fix dialogue and interpretative errors. By the end, we've chalked up an agreed-on version. During this time, I sometimes implant new facts—I give my adversary a leather bracelet he doesn't wear, and even have him fiddle with it nervously.

A month from the event, when asking kids to render the fight on a page, I'll mostly get fed this official account. What the group deems right almost always obliterates anybody's original recollections (except for those rare memory aces, who somehow cleave to their original intake). It's the power of groupthink, the basis of both family dynamics and most propaganda.

But worse than the groupthink that warps recall are the students' original, radical misjudgments. Poets and trained musicians seem mysteriously keen at nailing dialogue verbatim. But they can still flub tone or even misattribute who said what. I was the one saying, "We can work this out." But some credit Chris with the phrase as I jerked my elbow away. Some heard me exasperatedly sighing: "We *can't* work this out."

Who knows why half the class recalled my advancing toward Chris, when I either stood still or backed up? Even my inertia, if they observed it at all, got recorded in almost military terms: sentences such as "She held her ground" or "She was sturdy as a bulldog in her stance" appeared and I was likened to granite or steel. One year the memory star was a saxophonist and hip-hop DJ so convinced by our acting that he almost left his seat to stop the brute assaulting me. Yet even in possession of the facts, this kid wound up speculating as to "what Mary had done to make him attack her like this."

The observing students' innate prejudices shape how they view things. One year when I claimed the phone calls were from a doctor's office, a girl with a serious illness worried about me, while everybody else just resented my answering during class as a bratty move. One guy figured Chris and I had been sleeping together, and this kid half manufactured an insidious narrative of betrayal based on our body language. A girl who'd had a stalker figured Chris was one. Somebody else thought we were both high.

My unscientific, decades-long study proves even the best minds warp and blur what they see.

For all of memory's power to yank us back into an over-whelming past, it can also fail big time—both short-term (the lost vehicle in a parking lot, the name at the tip of your tongue) and long-term (we made out in high school?). That's why I always send my manuscripts out to folks I write about, because I don't trust my wiggly mind.

Memoirist Carolyn See recalled her husband bailing on her while she metaphorically held on to his leg. But her children and ex corrected her, saying she'd sent him packing. My friend David Carr of the *New York Times* tried to track down the facts about his most deranged coke-fiend years in *The Night of the Gun*, where he used investigative skills and a video camera to interview old running partners in Minneapolis. The highlight concerns a faceoff with a gun-toting maniac in an alley. The big reversal? It turned out Carr was the maniac wagging the gun. When he recounted that discovery to me years later, the discrepancy still set him back.

In fairness to David's memory, he was strung out at the time, but still. How can the mind get it so right, yet so wrong? Neurologist Jonathan Mink, MD, explained to me that with such intense memories as David's, we often record the emotion alone, all detail blurred into unreadable smear.

But lost memories are more our concern, and major lapses happen when episodic memory—events or experiences, feelings, times, places—and autobiographical memory (like episodic, but you-specific) move into semantic memory—thoughts or concepts, facts, meanings, knowledge. For me, fitting an episode into words squashes it down a little. Instead of lively sensations, I often wind up with a story containing an idea or opinion I may not even have anymore. These language memories I have to distrust a little.

In Mary McCarthy's *Memories of a Catholic Girlhood*, she writes of her son insisting that Mussolini was physically thrown off their bus in Hyannis, Massachusetts, in 1943, because the driver pulled over to the curb and "shouted the latest piece of news: 'They've thrown Mussolini out.' "

This yanks a laugh from you. Unless you're a memoirist. It makes me bite my already-chewed-down nails. The thought of misrepresenting someone or burning down his house with shitty recall wakes me up at night. I always tell my students that doubt runs through me every day I work, like the subway's third rail. So when people ask in challenging tones how I can possibly recall everything I've published, I often fess up, *Obviously I can't. But I've been able to bullshit myself that I do.* By this I mean, I do my best, which is limited by the failures of my so-called mind.

I come from a family of storytellers, and it's true that having a close group of folks retell events over and over better logs the narrative into long-term storage. But memorized language can also calcify what's in your head. Events grow stale when told by rote. Like old dough squeezed out of a pastry bag, the stories can feel too artificially shaped. Painful events told for humor can be drained of the real pathos or terror they first registered with.

And negotiated memories can be like a piece of writing clawed over by an editorial board—anything at all dubious gets deleted, and any particular point of view abolished. Anybody in a family knows how tyrannical groupthink can be.

Not long after my first memoir came out, my mother and sister started ringing up to recount scenes I'd written about using my language. As a younger sibling whose views tend to get heavily discounted, I might have registered this as a triumph—finally they get it! Instead I felt bereft. I had inadvertently become the official chronicler of our collective memories, and who knows what I was screwing up? Part of me longs for the old days when I couldn't open my mouth without hearing how something only happened a few times or wasn't that bad. In a warped way, being wrong was way better: it kept me folded more safely in the family delusion system.

2 | The Truth Contract Twixt Writer and Reader

*The whole journey is toward the truth, or toward
authenticity, agency, and freedom. How could it possibly
help to plant a lie in the middle of it?*

Edward St Aubyn

When I think of all the stiff pronouncements I've made demanding truth in memoir over the years, I'm inclined to hang my head. I sound like such a pious twit, the village vicar wagging her finger at writers pushing the limits of the form. Forgive me, I am not the art police. The wonderful thing about what comedian Stephen Colbert calls the "truthiness" of our era is that you can set any standard that blows up your coattail. Novelist Pam Houston claimed her novels are 82 percent true and ascribes that same percentage to her nonfiction—fair enough. I guess in today's literary landscape, you can choose your own percentage.

You can always hide behind the fiction label, as Truman Capote did (perhaps first) in 1966 with his "nonfiction novel," *In Cold Blood*; or as Philip Roth did in 1993 with his roman à clef *Operation Shylock*, which he published as fiction, while claiming it was God's own truth. (Ditto: my favorite parts of David Foster Wallace's *Infinite Jest* are more memoir than fiction.) Or you can make a general disclaimer, as John Berendt did in 1994, confessing that in *Midnight in the Garden of Good and Evil* he took "certain storytelling liberties, particularly having to do with the timing of events." I took this to mean that he telescoped time to move the story along. In fact, the book's murder—its central drama—occurred years before Berendt got there. So many scenes—including his own run-in with the victim and a popular cross-dressing character's role early in the investigation—are pure fiction. Which he at least admitted to, albeit somewhat slyly in back pages.

That's me speaking temperately as I can about other writers' artistic freedom, which I would go to the mat for. No writer can impose his own standards onto any other, nor claim to speak for the whole genre. I would defend anybody's right to move the line for veracity in memoir, though I'd argue the reader has a right to know. But my own humble practices wholly oppose making stuff up.

As a reader, I am way less temperate in my opinions. It niggles the hell out of me never to know exactly what parts the fabricators have fudged. In her recent interview in *The Believer*, Vivian Gornick claims to falter at truth telling, even in putatively nonfiction forms.

> I embellish stories all the time. I do it even when I'm supposedly telling the unvarnished truth. Things happen, and I realize that what actually happens is only partly a story, and I have to make the story. So

I lie. I mean, essentially—others would think I'm
lying. But you understand. It's irresistible to tell the
story. And I don't owe anybody the actuality. What is
the actuality? I mean, whose business is it?

Well, if I forked over a cover price for nonfiction, I consider
it my business. While it's great she owned up to her deceits,
it's hard to lend credence to any after-the-fact confession, especially one as vague or self-justifying as this one. It's as if after
lunch the deli guy quipped, "I put just a teaspoon of catshit in
your sandwich, but you didn't notice it at all." To my mind, a
small bit of catshit equals a catshit sandwich, unless I know
where the catshit is and can eat around it.

So here I stand with my little stick, attempting to draw a
line in the dirt for the sake of memoir's authenticity. Truth
may have become a foggy, fuzzy nether area. But untruth is
simple: making up events with the intention to deceive. Even
in this day of the photoshopped Facebook pic, that's not so
morally hard to gauge. You know the difference between a
vague memory and a clear one, and the vague ones either get
left out or labeled dubious. It's the clear ones that matter most
anyway, because they're the ones you've nursed and worried
over and talked through and wondered about your whole life.
And you're seeking the truth of memory—your memory and
character—not of unbiased history.

Forget how inventing stuff breaks a contract with the reader,
it fences the memoirist off from the deeper truths that only surface in draft five or ten or twenty. Yes, you can misinterpret—
happens all the time. "The truth ambushes you," Geoffrey Wolff
once said. (More on those hair-raising reversals in a later chapter.)

But unless you're looking at actual lived experience, the more profound meanings will remain forever shrouded. You'll never unearth the more complex truths, the ones that counter that convenient first take on the past. A memoirist forging false tales to support his more comfortable notions—or to pump himself up for the audience—never learns who he is. He's missing the personal liberation that comes from the examined life.

Liberation how? you might say. Why isn't it just as good to make up a version of events you can live with and stick to that? If your goal is to polish up a fake person you can sell to a public you perceive as dumb, the unexamined life will do perfectly well, thank you.

But whether you're a memoirist or not, there's a psychic cost for lopping yourself off from the past: it may continue to tug on you without your being aware of it. And lying about it can—for all but the most hardened sociopath—carve a lonely gap between your disguise and who you really are. The practiced liar also projects her own manipulative, double-dealing facade onto everyone she meets, which makes moving through the world a wary, anxious enterprise. It's hard enough to see what's going on without forcing yourself to look through the wool you've pulled over your own eyes.

To watch someone scrutinize a painful history in depth—which I've done as teacher and editor and while working with former drunks trying to clear up ancient crimes—is to witness not inconsiderable pain. You have to lance a boil and suffer its stench as infection drains off. Yet all the scrupulous self-examinations over time I've been witness to—whether on the page or off—always ended with acceptance and relief. For the more haunted among us, only looking back at the past can permit it finally to become past.

. . .

How does telling the truth help a reader's experience, though? Let's say you had an awful childhood—tortured and mocked and starved every day—hit hard with belts and hoses, etc. You could write a repetitive, duller-than-a-rubber-knife misery memoir. But would that be "true"? And true to how you keep it boxed up now, or to lived experience back then? Back then, those same abusers probably fed you something, or you'd have died—and maybe you felt grateful for their crumbs, or furious, or even unworthy. No doubt you were either given false hope, or you cooked up futile schemes to win them over, to improve your lot. Or you fought back and rebelled. Or you disassociated much of the time. Or some awful part of you admired their strength, and you fantasized about being as strong yourself. It's the disparities in your childhood, your life between ass-whippings, that throws past pain into stark relief for a reader. Without those places of hope, the beatings become too repetitive—maybe they'd make a dramatic read for a while, but single-note tales seldom bear rereading.

The most fastidious writers do overhaul their versions based on later information. When Jon Krakauer was stumbling around oxygen-deprived and brain-damaged on Mount Everest, he misidentified people he ran into in a blinding blizzard—mistakes he corrected in later versions of *Into Thin Air* (1997). I also know Krakauer drives his publishers crazy revamping stories decades old, as he recently did when he spent ten years learning organic chemistry well enough to revise his idea of what seed poisoned the protagonist of *Into the Wild* (1996). Krakauer spends more time rechecking and revising than almost any nonfiction writer I know, which says much about his devotion to getting things right.

My friend Frank McCourt's mother denied stuff like sleeping with her own cousin, but who wouldn't? Certainly that outrage didn't make or break *Angela's Ashes*. Way worse in terms of maternal malfeasance was letting an underfed girl die in bed, which Mother McCourt never denied. What would motivate Frank, who loved his mother, to make up the incest if it weren't true? Oh—and Kathryn Harrison's father, a fundamentalist Christian minister at the time, denied having sex with her: no surprise. You have to suspect these obviously self-interested detractors. Other than them, I haven't heard a single credible story from a memoirist pal about family faultfinding.

Lest you think I'm some crazed lone gunman for the truth, I offer this fact: the autobiographers whose practices I've admired up close over the decades have—almost to a one—shown their manuscripts around prepublication. And none faced major challenges to their versions based on family complaint. My sample includes Geoffrey and Tobias Wolff and Lucy Grealy, and former students Koren Zailckas and Cheryl Strayed. Also, yours truly. I was asked by a minor character to cut a tangential anecdote in my last book. Other than that minor blip, no one I know has overhauled pages based on family outrage. But interviewers and audiences are gobsmacked when I mention this. No one believes memoirists aren't constantly assaulted by detractors and naysayers and lawsuits.

How is that possible? Well, as Frank Conroy said of his mother's response to *Stop-Time*, "She felt it was my version of events." The best memoirists stress the subjective nature of reportage. Doubt and wonder come to stand as part of the story.

We also have to distinguish between memories wrangled

over at the supper table and memoirs combed over and revised dozens of times before being published. Everybody's personal history is jam packed with long, wheedling family arguments in which every reporter represents a personal view of history as irrefutable reality. Such arguments are private and informal. And we tend to argue as if we're right for stone certain. We've all wallowed in such never-resolved mudholes. Common memory rifts involve either (1) unknowable interpretation—someone's inner intent or motives; or (2) chronology—dates or how long something went on or how often; and/or (3) disagreements about place—where something went down. We all screw such facts up, it's true, either unintentionally or in heated crusade to prove our private takes on family history. Many a loved one has engaged in hyperbole or stretched the bounds of evidence or dug in her heels to prove a point that's wrong.

But ask yourself, how many of your clan would just flat out make up stuff that everybody knows is bullshit, then publish it? Publishing lies requires a whole different level of sociopathy. For veracity's sake, it doesn't cost a memoirist the reader's confidence either to skip over the half-remembered scene or to replicate her own psychic uncertainty—"This part is blurry." Any decent comp teacher schools you to work in the realms of *maybe* and *perhaps*. The great memoirist enacts recall's fuzzy form. That's why we trust her.

As we've lost faith in old authorities, our confidence in objective truth has likewise eroded. Science and scripture and church doctrine were once judged unassailable founts of truth. History was told from the viewpoint of the victors—cowboys good, Native Americans bad. We've learned to question the Pentagon report and the firm presidential denial. Histories and biographies often open with "positioning essays" explaining the writer's innate prejudices. And while formerly sacred sources of truth like history and statistics have lost ground, the subjective tale has garnered new territory. That's partly why memoir is in its ascendancy—not because it's not corrupt, but because the best ones openly confess the nature of their corruption.

The master memoirist creates such a personal interior space, with memories pieced together, that the reader never loses sight of the enterprise's tentative nature. Maxine Hong Kingston and Michael Herr don't manufacture authoritative, third-person, I-am-a-camera views. Their books don't masquerade as fact. They let you in on how their own prejudices mold memory's sifter. By transcribing the mind so its edges show, a writer constantly reminds the reader that he's not watching crisp external events played from a digital archive. It's the speaker's truth alone. In this way, the form constantly disavows the rigors of objective truth.

So how have memoirists' families reacted? Toby Wolff claimed he was corrected on small points, mostly of chronology, but basically stuck by his memories, which remained uncorrected by family. So a dog his mother found adorable he persists in calling ugly.

Geoffrey Wolff felt honor-bound by an idea of history: "Readers are very sophisticated," he wrote. "They understand that a promise has been made." But he was also suspicious of those unshakable icons of evidence for the average historian—documents like letters and tax returns and diaries.

> Documents are tricky things too. And I was dealing
> with my father—a systematic liar. You can't report

annual income on the basis of his 1040 form. And I'm looking at a copy of his resume right now. It lists the head of the CIA as a reference, cites degrees from Yale and the Sorbonne.

To give a more innocent example, how many of us have our actual weights on our drivers' licenses? And yet a historian might draw on such records—or letters or diaries—as authoritative facts.

Bending the truth wasn't always part of the autobiographer's tool kit. In the middle of the last century, when Mary McCarthy published *Catholic Girlhood*, memoirists weren't even supposed to cobble up dialogue from memory. Her nonfiction standards were those for histories and biographies and journalism—forms then still held to be fairly irrefutable. Whether we were more gullible or more secretive or the standards more rigorous then, I can't say—probably all three.

So while McCarthy claims her book "lays a claim to being historical—that is, much of it can be checked," she apologizes in six long italicized streaks for her then-edgy liberties, including innocent mistakes: "*But perhaps we didn't 'know' it was the flu.*" Even to put *know* in quotes back then acted as a hedge against the then almost-inviolable standards of precision that a memoirist may feel free of today. Here are some of McCarthy's major apologies:

1. On reconstructing dialogue: *"Many a time in the course of doing these memoirs, I have wished I were writing fiction. The temptation to invent had been very strong, particularly when I remember the substance of an event but not the particulars. Sometimes I have yielded,*

as in the case of conversations. . . . They are mostly fic-
tional. . . . Only a few single sentences stand out. Quo-
tation marks indicate that a conversation to this general
effect took place, but I do not vouch for the exact words"
(emphasis mine).

2. On proper names: "*I have not given the right names to*
   my teachers or fellow students. . . . But all these people are
   real, they are not composite portraits. In the case of my
   near relations, I have given real names [as with] neigh-
   bors, servants and friends."

3. On the nature of her memory: "*There are several du-*
   bious points in this memoir. . . . Just when we got the flu
   seems to be arguable. According to newspaper accounts,
   we contracted it on the trip. This conflicts with the story
   that Uncle Harry and Aunt Zula brought it with them.
   My present memory supports the idea that someone was
   sick before we left, but perhaps we didn't 'know' it was
   [that lethal] flu."

4. Or on the nature of the false, implanted memory:
   "*We did not see [our father draw a revolver]. . . . I heard*
   the story from my other grandmother. When she told me,
   I had the feeling that I almost remembered it. That is, my
   mind promptly supplied me with a picture of it."

The memoirist's truth has been devolving (or evolving)
since *Girlhood*. In McCarthy's later book, *Intellectual Memoirs*
(1992), our culture's truth transformation was nearing comple-
tion. She talks almost scornfully about "the fetishism of fact,"
but in *Girlhood*, she's still heeling to that notion.

Whatever your deal with the reader, I argue for stating it up
front, like Harry Crews in his 1978 *A Childhood: The Biography*

of a Place. His concept of "truth" is way more wiggly than the Wolffs' and mine, but he admits it. With his first sentence, he embraces gossip and hearsay and all manner of apocrypha.

> My first memory is of a time ten years before I was born and takes place where I have never been and involves my daddy whom I never knew.

Lest you disparage this type of gossip, the gospels are probably all stories passed on by folks who heard them from other folks. Without other people's stories, Crews cannot hook himself to his long-lost ghost father, and we embrace his method partly from empathy for his yearning for his old man—and partly because it's all so fun to read.

> Did what I have set down here as memory actually happen? Did the two men say what I have recorded, think what I have said they thought? I do not know, nor do I any longer care. My knowledge of my daddy came entirely from the stories I have been told about him.

Crews claims that whatever errors in detail he may make, the stories he's been told remain true "in spirit." Whatever that means, it does scoop out a fairly big escape hatch for somebody writing nonfiction.

Plus Crews trains us in his methods of amplification early— not just through his use of rumor, but by drawing on his child's imaginative point of view, as when he has a long talk with his dog, Sam, early on.

> "If you was any kind of man atall, you wouldn't snap at them gnats and eat them flies the way you do," I said.

"It ain't a thing in the world the matter with eatin
gnats and flies," he said.

"It's how come people treat you like a dog," I said.
"You could probably come on in the house like other
folks if it weren't for eatin flies and gnats like you do."

So Crews lets us know that his path vis-à-vis external veracity or reporting history is undulating as a snake's.

Later in the book, he writes about an injury that just could not
have gone down as described. He's playing pop-the-whip during
hog scalding time—when whole carcasses are dropped in boiling water so their bristles can be scraped off. Crews claims he
landed in the boiling water "beside a scalded, floating hog."

I reached over and touched my right hand with my
left, and the whole thing came off like a wet glove. I
mean, the skin on the top of the wrist and the back of
my hand, along with the fingernails, all just turned
loose and slid on down to the ground. I could see my
fingernails lying in the little puddle of flesh made on
the ground in front of me.

So devoted am I to this undervalued memoir that I phoned a
doctor pal in a burn unit to be sure whether a kid could suffer
such an injury without crazy scarring or loss of limb. Of course
he couldn't.

But hyperbole to the point of unreality fits with Crews's
Georgia cracker milieu, which can trace its roots both to southern gothic at its most violent and grotesque and to tall tales from
around the campfire, such as Mark Twain's celebrated jumping-
frog story where in order to win a bet the gambler Jim Smiley
did "foller a straddle bug to Mexico." Hyperbole often reflects
a culture's excesses in savagery and appetite, and at one point,

Crews quips, "Anything worth doing is worth over-doing." (The unspoken battle cry of many an alcoholic such as myself.)

Since anybody's handling of the truth derives from her nature, and I know nobody's nature so well as my own, I feel obliged to detail my own practice, though I do so with no more authority than any other memoirist.

Though, like Crews, I quote wild tales and rumors from my cracker past, I just have zero talent for making stuff up. While I adore the short story form, any time I tried penning one myself, everybody was either dead by page two, or morphed back into the person they'd actually evolved from in memory. Stuck in an airport with an uncharged reading device, I'll pop for crap nonfiction before a crap novel.

Early on, I was lied to—often and with conviction—kicked off by two phrases: "I'm not drunk" (most always a lie) and "Oh, don't worry; everything's fine," which was true just often enough to mess with my head. In high school, both the fake notes my sister forged to skip school and her excuses for breaking dates with boys held the seeds of unwritten novels, and one of the sayings that still graces her holiday table would make a worthy family crest: "A good lie well told and stuck to is often better than the truth."

All this quite literally made me crazy. I grew up not trusting my perceptions, and buying Freud's theory that the truth would free me, I set out on a lifelong quest to figure out what the hell happened in my childhood. While my mother threatened suicide when I initially tried to probe her past, by my mid-twenties, she gave in. Unearthing the truth led to radical healing in my otherwise fractured clan, and she died sober and much loved.

For me, making stuff up—as I first did in trying to tell my story in novel form five years before I embraced memoir—put me off the scent of what I was born to tell. Even trying to use pseudonyms messed with my head something awful. Some inner corrector kept saying, *But that's not John, it's Bob.* So in rough drafts, I had to work with real names, which got changed in a global search-and-replace only at the end.

One reason I send manuscripts out to friends and family in advance is: I often barely believe myself, for I grew up suspicious of my own perceptions. Plus my kinfolk had changed their stories so many times, I was hoping their signing off on pages would finally end my own lifetime's speculation.

Long ago, when I was younger and broker and looked easier to boss around, a publishing executive tried to nudge me into inventing a scene in my first book when I say good-bye to my mother. "The reader has to know how that went down at that moment. . . ." But I remembered zip about the scene and wound up guessing about it instead:

> Mother must have squawked about our leaving. She
> would have yelled or wept or folded up drunk and
> sulking. I recall no such scene. . . . The French doors
> on that scene never swung open. . . . Mother herself
> was clipped from my memory. She did promise
> vaguely to come for us soon, but I can't exactly hear
> her saying that.

And here's the kicker: I'd now guess that she felt liberated once we left—such is the nature of time reversing an opinion. When I was younger and Mother alive, we both found it easier to pretend she'd fought for us. But I never actually saw Mother fighting for our company—she always much preferred the wild freedom of solitude. Were I starting the book over, I'd guess she didn't mind our absence overmuch.

Though *The Liars' Club* rang true to me when I wrote it, from this juncture it seems to have sprung from a state of loving delusion about my family. In those days, I still enjoyed a child's desperate tendency to put sparkles on my whole tribe. Were I writing that story today, I'd be less generous to them while perhaps shining more empathy on my younger self. Whether age has granted me more wholesome care for the girl I was, or whether life's ravages have ground down my heart so I'm more self-centered, I can't say. Am I healthily less codependent or a bigger bitch? You could argue either way. Although I'd fix a wrong date or point of fact for the book to correct it as written record, I couldn't alter any major take on the past without redoing the whole tome. The self who penned that book formed the filter for those events. I didn't fabricate stuff, but today, other scenes I'd add might tell a less forgiving story.

Which brings me to the wellsprings where a writer's biggest "lies" bubble up—interpretation. I still try to err on the side of generosity toward any character. Like I mention Mother throwing my birthday lasagna at my daddy in one of the zillion fights that felt like my fault, but I also mention her cleaning it up after he was gone and lighting candles on a German chocolate cake—a scene that, if left out, would've skewed her into seeming worse than she in fact was. Anne Fadiman writes about a nineteenth-century sailor who comes home to a starving family at Christmas with a bushel of oranges. He locks himself in a room and devours them solo while his kids scratch at the door. He's an asshole, right? Until you learn he had scurvy.

Metaphorically speaking, I always make room for any evidence of scurvy in my characters, any mitigating ailments. In my last memoir, I couldn't report a malicious quip from my ex-husband without mentioning that he never spoke to me that way. Maybe that's why it stayed carved in my psyche: it was out of character. A writer whose point of view was closer inside the past might only concentrate on feeling wounded by the insult without tacking on that fact, because it could jar the reader from the instant. Mostly, I try to keep the focus on myself and my own peccadilloes.

For the record, here are the liberties I've used, which all seem fairly common now:

1. Re-creating dialogue. I've often said, "The conversation went something like this," but most readers presume as much. Also, by not using quotation marks in later books, I seek to keep the reader more "inside" my experience—the subjective nature eschews the standards of history, I think.

2. Changing names to protect the innocent. Most of my friends had a hoot choosing their pseudonyms.

3. Altering the name of the town. Most minor characters like the sheriff and school principal I don't bother to track down. They might be dead, but if they are alive, I don't want the responsibility of perhaps misremembering them.

4. Blurring details of somebody's appearance for the sake of their privacy. I've only done this many times for minor characters—a mayor, say. But for the neighborhood rapist in *Liar's Club*, I didn't want folks in my hometown to mistakenly blame one of the local delinquents. I gave the culprit braces, which nobody in our neighborhood had, and changed a few other things.

With *Lit*, I hoped my ex-husband would vet the manuscript pages, but when I spoke to him in advance, he claimed to prefer being blurry.

5. Moving back and forth through time when appropriate and giving info you didn't have at the time, which breaks point of view. (If your next-door neighbor turned out to be, say, Ted Bundy, you might mention that in parentheses because you know the reader would care to know.) It's still apparent when I do this that I speak from another time.

6. Telescoping time: "Seventeen years later, Daddy had a stroke. . . ." Or using one episode to stand for all of seventh grade. The action points for a given period represent it wholesale. I skip dull parts.

7. Shaping a narrative. Of course, the minute you write about one thing instead of another, you've begun to leave stuff out, which you could argue is falsifying. What was major to you might have been a blip on somebody else's radar.

8. Stopping to describe something in the midst of a heated scene, when I probably didn't observe it consciously at that instant. This is perhaps the biggest lie I ever tell. I do so because I am constantly trying to re-create the carnal world as I lived it, so I keep concocting an experience for a reader. I have taken that liberty, but because I'm Catholic, I feel guilty about it.

9. Temporarily changing something to protect a friend at her request. My friend Meredith had been a habitué of asylums, but she still didn't want me to publish a school scene of her razoring at her wrist, because it would torment her aging mother. She agreed to let a mutual friend stand in for her, so the suicidal friend is Stacy in the first edition and Meredith in later ones.

10. Recounting old fantasies. My inner life is much bigger than my outer life. And some fantasies from the past seem gaudily true. 'Course, I say they're only fancies, not fact. In *Liars' Club* I also made up two of the tall tales, which are meant to be bullshit anyway.

11. Putting in scenes I didn't witness but only heard about—though I admit as much. From *Lit*: "So vivid is the story of mother's final drunk with Harold—so painterly in its grotesque detail—that I take the liberty of recounting it as if I were there, for a good story told often enough puts you in rooms never occupied."

12. Vis-à-vis interpretation: be generous and fair when you can; when you can't, admit your disaffinity. My general idea is to keep the focus on myself and my own struggles, not speculate on other people's motives, and not concoct events and characters out of whole cloth.

3 | Why Not to Write a Memoir: Plus a Pop Quiz to Protect the Bleeding & Box Out the Rigid

If you are silent about your pain, they'll kill you and say you enjoyed it.

Zora Neale Hurston

Asking me how to write a memoir is a little like saying, "I really want to have sex, where do I start?" What one person fantasizes about would ruin the romance for another. It depends on how you're constructed inside and out, hormone levels, psychology. Or it's like saying, "I want a makeover, how should I look?" A Goth girl's not inclined to lime-green Fair Isle sweaters, and a preppy scorns black lipstick.

I've said it's hard. Here's how hard: everybody I know who wades deep enough into memory's waters drowns a little. Between chapters of *Stop-Time*, Frank Conroy stayed drunk for weeks. Two hours after Carolyn See finished her first draft of *Dreaming*, she collapsed with viral meningitis, which gave her double vision: "It was my brain's way of saying, 'You've been looking where you shouldn't be looking.' " Martin Amis reported a suffocating enervation while working on *Experience*. Writing fiction, however taxing, usually left him some buoyancy at day's end; his memoir about his father drained him. Jerry Stahl relapsed while writing about his heroin addiction in *Permanent Midnight*.

I used to crumble to the floor of my study afternoons, like a long-distance trucker. I'd have to claw my way out of sleep. When I once asked my shrink if I was repressing some memory, he said, "Nah, you're just really tired." I also remember turning the last page of a manuscript with my editor and feeling fever crawl up my face—103 degrees. I had pneumonia, which I'd never had before.

Here are some excellent reasons not to do this, and following that a pop quiz to gauge your readiness:

1. If you're psychologically hectored by the nattering voice of some scold about how wrong this is, maybe wait till you find some balance. You can care what people think, so long as you're not brutally squeezed by it.
2. If you have a bad memory, give it up. Many people ask me how to recall the past, and I say if they don't, they're lucky—get a real job.
3. If the events you're writing about are less than seven or eight years past, you might find it harder than you think. Distance frees us of our former ego's vanities and lets us see deeper into events.
4. Also if you're young, you might wanna wait. Most of us are still soft as clay before thirty-five. (I know, Dave Eggers was about twelve when he wrote his wildly successful *Heartbreaking Work of Staggering Genius*, but he's an exception.)

5. If you're doing it for therapy, go hire somebody to talk to. Your psychic health should matter more than your literary production.

6. If you want revenge, hire a lawyer. Or find a way to have fun with it. I have a friend who got a nasty review, then received the reviewer's book in the mail for a possible review from him. His reply? "I took it on the back porch and put a bullet through its head." He shot the book and mailed it back to the publisher. Buy darts and a dartboard. Literature's for something else: the reader.

7. Don't write about people you hate (though Hubert Selby claims you can do it with great love). Ditto: don't write about a divorce you're going through.

8. If your writing affects a group of people—a class or race—be sure you're ready for any fallout. Maxine Hong Kingston got slightly fried by the Chinese community; McCourt took grief from the Irish.

9. If you're a right-fighter, somebody who never apologizes or changes her mind, you don't have the fluid nature to twig to the deep river of truth when the spirit draws your forked stick.

10. Related to the above: if you can't rewrite, give it up. You need to be able to rethink and correct the easy interpretation.

If you still want to proceed, you want to be sure you can handle all you might feel. Pass this quiz, and I knight your shoulders in blessing with my own fine-line, razor-point pen.

Let's say something pseudo-awful has befallen you—a safe bet for any human unit thinking about a memoir. And you imagine you'll write the very worst scene "down the road," after you've gotten your feet wet. You'll work up to it. Let's face it: you dread this scene as the rich dread tax time, as demons dread Jesus. It's a haunter.

You're going to write it now.

Don't get me wrong: your goal is not to finish these pages. The opposite. This draft will land in a folder you keep. I want you to suffer through sitting in a room for some hours with your worst memories. But you'll start with a centering exercise in an attempt to get underneath your normal ego and into some deeper place, more receptive to the truth. Meditation as a technique to loosen creative powers fills boatloads of books. There are millions of techniques: counting your breaths one to ten, following your breath, a mantra, visualization, studying a passage of sacred writing.

In getting tough-guy undergrads to meditate, I found the story of Zen basketball master Phil Jackson's *Sacred Hoops* useful. Students who'd otherwise refuse to close their eyes and get woo-woo in class went along behind Jackson's example.

Phil writes about playing as a young man from a warrior's ego—all rage for dominance. But in the NBA, as he reaches the far edge of his natural physical talent, he chooses to cultivate a mental edge. Through Zen meditation, Jackson starts to notice how much noise is in his head during a game, including anger ("That #$%^& Chamberlain. Next time he's dead meat.") and self-blame ("Phil, a sixth-grader could've made that shot!").

> The litany was endless. However the simple act of becoming mindful in the frenzied parade of thoughts, paradoxically, began to quiet my mind down. . . .
> Yogi Berra once said about baseball: "How can you think and hit at the same time?" The same is true with basketball, except everything's happening much faster.

The same is true of writing. To tap in to your deepest talent, you need to seek out a calm, restful state of mind where your head isn't defending your delicate ego and your heart can bloom open a little. For me, my mind is constantly checking where I am in line—comparing myself to others, or even to a former self, racing, fretting, conniving to get ahead. But underneath that is another self that quietly notices all that. A friend called to say she was going crazy once, and I said, "Who's noticing that?" You want to get next to that quiet, noticer self as a starting place.

Just apply your ass to the chair (as someone wise once said, a writer's only requirement) and for fifteen or twenty minutes, practice getting your attention out of your head, down to some wider expanse in your chest or solar plexus—a place less self-conscious or skittery or scared. The idea is to unclench your mind's claws. So don't judge how your thoughts might jet around at first. Eventually you'll start identifying a little bit with that detached, watcher self and less with your prattling head.

You're seeking enough quiet to let the Real You into your mind. Inspiration—the drawing into the body of some truth-giving spirit ready to walk observantly through the doors of the past. Then, with eyes still closed, approach the memory you're scared to set down. Start by composing the scene in carnal terms—by which I mean using sensory impressions, not sexual ones. Smell is the oldest sense—even one-celled animals without spinal cords can smell—and it cues emotional memory like nothing else. If you can conjure the aroma of where you are—fresh-cut grass or lemon furniture oil, say—you're half-way there.

What can you see, hear, touch, taste? What do you have on?

Is the cloth rough or smooth? If you're on the beach, there's a salt spray, and you need a sweater. In the trench, sweat snails down your spine. What taste is in your mouth?

I always liken the state I'm in before I write to waking too early to rise and looking for a wormhole to corkscrew down into that more honest place. You want a clear sense memory, a treasured (or despised) object. And most of all, you want your old body. Your cold hand wrapped around a jelly glass of grape juice. That toy monkey with the switch on its back that banged cymbals and—when smacked on its head—hissed at you. You need a point of physical and psychic connection, a memory you'd swear by to start with. Then allow the memory to play itself. It won't be video footage, of course, only jump cuts, snippets, an idea here and there, an image.

Now open your eyes. If you're doing this right, the whole thing should've been arrestingly vivid, maybe even a little awful. Many students open their eyes with tears welling up.

Sit a minute and let all this wash past. You should feel like you've been somewhere. If you're really lucky, you found a way to occupy your former self, looking out of that face at your much younger hands. Congrats. That's impressive. Most of us get a few snippets and glimpses.

Now, here's the pop quiz part: can you be in that place without falling apart? If you're sobbing with shoulders shaking and big tusks of snot coming out of your face, the answer may be no. Call a pal, book a massage, go for a walk. You're not ready to occupy this space for years on end. Yet.

If you couldn't see much or you felt nothing, you may not be ready, either. Or if you can only feel one thing, self-righteous rage—unless it's a book about a larger atrocity (i.e., you're a Sudanese "lost boy")—this may not be your forte.

Those of you who felt a living emotional connection to the past that struck you as real, those who've been somewhere, who brim with feeling and may even be crying, but are not devastated—come on in.

Now try writing some pages to serve as later notes. Because you're not yet sure of voice or anything else, you're free from the need to squash in all manner of background information, explaining what year it is, etc. That stuff will just get you back in your head and drive you nuts. You're free to write as if all that stuff is in the reader's head already. It will be, by the time you get to this part of the book.

You might ask, though, who are you writing for? Lots of people say, "I write for myself." I am way less cool. I tend to imagine a writer pal I look up to, maybe a former teacher; or my son; or even my dead priest. That helps me think clearly about what order information goes in. Again, if you were telling a therapist or a friend at lunch, you'd know right away what data went where.

If you do have a reader in mind, maybe set down the scene in letter form, mustering as much carnal detail as you can feel. At the same time you're going to try to describe your insides—either now as you watch this or then as you were in it, it doesn't matter which point of view. And if you go back and forth to your adult self, show how that feels, to slip from present tense into a memory.

And here are some questions that might nudge you along. What were you trying to get, and how? Which ways worked? Which didn't? If it's a particularly awful memory for your character, you have to be sure not to make it more awful than it was. Many of us disassociate or check out during awful times, so maybe you want to convey that to the reader. The memoirist's job is not to add explosive whammies on every page, but to help the average person come in. Otherwise, the reader will gawk at you like somebody on *Springer*, or she'll pity you—in both cases, you lose some authority. The book becomes too much about your feeling and not enough about the reader's.

Finally, put it aside. Put it out of your head at least a week. You want it to set up like jello. And when you pick it back up, ask yourself, What haven't I said? How might someone else involved have seen it differently?

And most of all, how am I afraid of appearing? Go beyond looking bad or good. Is there posturing or self-consciousness you could cut or correct or confess and make use of?

At the nadir of my confidence as a writer, I despaired of ever finishing *Lit*. I considered selling my apartment to give the advance money back. Then a Jesuit pal asked me, quite simply, What would you write if you weren't afraid? I honestly didn't know at first. But I knew finding the answer would unlock the writing for me.

Now you may not know what you'd write if you weren't afraid. I seldom do. It's a moment-to-moment struggle. But if you're passionate to find out, then you're ready. God help you.

4 | A Voice Conjures the Human Who Utters It

I believe that when the last ding-dong of doom has clanged and faded from the last worthless rock hanging tideless in the last red and dying evening, that even then there will still be one more sound: that of [man's] puny inexhaustible voice, still talking.

William Faulkner

Each great memoir lives or dies based 100 percent on voice. It's the delivery system for the author's experience—the big bandwidth cable that carries in lustrous clarity every pixel of someone's inner and outer experiences. Each voice is cleverly fashioned to highlight a writer's individual talent or way of viewing the world. A memoirist starts off fumbling—jotting down facts, recounting anecdotes. It may take a writer hundreds of rough trial pages for a way of speaking to start to emerge unique to himself and his experience, but when he does, both carnal and interior experiences come back with clarity, and the work gains an electrical charge. For the reader, the voice has to exist from the first sentence.

Because memoir is such a simple form, its events can come across—in the worst books—as thinly rendered and haphazard. But if the voice has a high enough voltage, it will carry the reader through all manner of assholery and tangent because it almost magically conjures in her imagination a fully realized human. We kind of think the voice *is* the narrator. It certainly helps if the stories are riveting, but a great voice renders the dullest event remarkable.

The secret to any voice grows from a writer's finding a tractor beam of inner truth about psychological conflicts to shine the way. While an artist consciously constructs a voice, she chooses its elements because they're natural expressions of character. So above all, a voice has to sound like the person wielding it—the super-most interesting version of that person ever—and grow from her core self.

Pretty much all the great memoirists I've met sound on the page like they do in person. If the page is a mask, you rip it off only to find that the writer's features exactly mold to the mask's form, with nary a gap between public and private self. These writers' voices make you feel close to—almost inside—their owners. Who doesn't halfway consider even a fictional narrator like Huck Finn or Scout a pal?

The voice should permit a range of emotional tones—too wiseass, and it denies pathos; too pathetic, and it's shrill. It sets and varies distance from both the material and the reader—from cool and diffident to high-strung and close. The writer doesn't choose these styles so much as he's born to them, based on who he is and how he experienced the past.

Voice isn't just a manner of talking. It's an operative mindset and way of perceiving that naturally stems from feeling oneself alive inside the past. That's why self-awareness is so key. The writer who's lived a fairly unexamined life—someone who has a hard time reconsidering a conflict from another point of view—may not excel at fashioning a voice because her defensiveness stands between her and what she has to say. Also, we naturally tend to superimpose our present selves onto who we were before, and that can prevent us from recalling stuff that doesn't shore up our current identities. Or it can warp understanding to fit more comfortable interpretations. All those places we misshape the past have to be 'fessed to, and such reflections and uncertainties have to find expression in voice.

You cut a contract early on to offer up the deepest perceptions you can muster without preening and posturing. Other writers may work otherwise, but every great memoirist I ever talked to sounded cursed to face up to real events. That's just the nature of the enterprise. Truth works a trip wire that permits the book to explode into being.

If the reader intuits some deception or kink in the writer's psyche that he can't admit to, it erodes the scribbler's authority. This drives a reader from the page, putting the writer in competition with Chubby Hubby ice cream and the TV remote—tough contests to win.

However you charm people in the world, you should do so on the page. A lot of great writers rebuke charm, and I don't mean the word to conjure a snake charmer pulling off a trick with a poor dumb animal whose fangs have been torn out. Too many writers relate to their readers that way, which results in some dull, hermetic books written just to satisfy the artist's preening ego. *Charm* is from the Latin *carmen*: to sing. By "charm," I mean sing well enough to hold the reader in thrall. Whatever people like about you in the world will manifest itself on the page. What drives them crazy will keep you humble. You'll need both sides of yourself—the beautiful and the beastly—to hold a reader's attention.

Sadly, without a writer's dark side on view—the pettiness and vanity and schemes—pages give off the whiff of bullshit. People may like you because you're warm, but you can also be quick to anger or too intense. Your gift for charm and confidence hides a gift for scheming and deceit. You're withdrawn and deep but also slightly scornful of others. A memoirist must cop to it all, which means routing out the natural ways you try to masquerade as somebody else—nicer, smarter, faster, funnier. All the good lines can't be the memoirist's.

Richard Wright's *Black Boy*, published in pre–civil rights America, seems to shun charm and speak with a bitterness he paid dear for. That refusal to pander forms the core of his talent—a ruthless, unblinking gaze that reports to us with often barely tamped-down fury.

It was Wright who started the American memoir craze of the last century with the publication of *Black Boy* in 1945. (The book gushed out of him in 1943.) He was followed closely by other smash hits: Thomas Merton's *Seven-Storey Mountain* (1948), Vladimir Nabokov's *Speak, Memory* (1951), and Mary McCarthy's *Memories of a Catholic Girlhood* (1957). Nabokov was publishing excerpts in France starting in 1936, and McCarthy in the *New Yorker* in 1946, but for my money, it was Wright who first won an audience in book length without being wildly famous first. Wright started shaping the form as we think of it today. (The next generation featured Maya Angelou and Frank Conroy, who no doubt learned from the aforementioned first-timers.)

Booker T. Washington's *Up from Slavery* had previously been a national best seller, but Washington had been a major figure before. Wright was the first African American to ride from oblivion onto the *New York Times* best-seller list. Not the last, though, for Malcolm X (1965) and Angelou (1969) bobbed in his wake. As a little white girl in segregated Texas, I found such books showed me racism as we were all still gagging on it. Today I even wonder if those memoirs didn't partly fuel the civil rights movement. Without them, black experience would've been rendered solely in sociopolitical speak. Wright's refusal to shuffle Uncle Tom–like down the page trying to cull favor was a revolutionary act at his time in history, and it reads as true in that context. Of course, his voice can also transport with its poetry:

> Each event spoke with a cryptic tongue. And the moments of living slowly released their coded meanings. There was the wonder I felt when I first saw a brace of mountainlike, spotted, black-and-white horses clopping down a dusty road through clouds of powdered clay.
>
> There was the delight I caught in seeing long straight rows of red and green vegetables stretching away in the sun to the bright horizon.

But such tender moments stand in stark relief to the brutal facts of the Jim Crow South and segregated Chicago. He starts off *Black Boy* with a distracted, aimless rage; deciding to set the family house on fire:

> My idea was growing, blooming. Now I was wondering just how the long fluffy white curtains

would look if I lit a bunch of [broom] straws on fire and held it under them. Would I try it? Sure.

After this, he's beaten almost to death by his mother and takes a hallucinatory stretch in bed. Soon after that, he finds a way to defy and infuriate his bullying father. Awakened into a fury by a mewing kitten, the old man tells Richard to shut it up: "Kill that damn thing!" And the boy does.

Wright depicts killing the kitten with chilling detachment. After arguing his father into the ground about the "rightness" of having killed the animal, he notes:

> I had had my first triumph over my father. I had made him believe I had taken his words literally. He could not punish me now without risking his authority. . . . I had made him know that I felt he was cruel and I had done it without his punishing me.

Wright's lawyerly case eschews all moral piety, laying bare the ruthless scrap for truth and turf—even in his family—that he was born to. At a time when his American publishers could cudgel him into changing the book's title from *American Hunger* to *Black Boy*—thus reducing a visionary's label into a racial slur—his voice above all speaks with a sense of unblinking veracity, refusing any soft focus. He's one of few memoirists who can pull it off. (German novelist Thomas Bernhard's *Gathering Evidence* and Graves's *Good-Bye to All That* also come across as bitter: that tone, which might grate coming from other writers, feels like the inevitable cost of their truths.)

• • •

In my experience teaching in a hyperselective grad program, pretty much any truth written deeply and with enough clarity and candor to allow emotional range winds up fascinating me. I'm not sure just any scribbler could win my praise writing lived experiences, but our students seem fairly adroit at cobbling up unique voices that hold me in thrall.

And the more memorable the voice, the *truer* a book sounds, because you never lose sight of the narrator cobbling together *his* truth—not everybody's agreed-on version. Or is it the truer a book, the better the voice?

Great memoirs *sound* like distinct persons and also cover a broad range of feelings. The glib jokester becomes as tedious and as unbelievable as the whiner.

This talent for truth includes a voice's bold ability to render events we find unbelievable elsewhere. On the first page of Hilary Mantel's *Giving Up the Ghost*—for my money a book as worship-worthy as any of her prizewinning fiction—we hear about her encounters with the spirit world. On a staircase, she passes through a shimmer in the air that contains a ghost: "I know it is my stepfather's ghost coming down. Or, to put it in a way acceptable to most people, I 'know' it is my stepfather's ghost." First off, she states the mystical experience as simple fact, but because she knows many readers in our skeptical culture will adjudge her bonkers, she spends a subsequent sentence traveling to where those readers' more rationalist belief systems hold sway. She rephrases, putting *know* in quotes. So she starts inside her mystical experience, then briefly jogs to where the dubious reader stands prepared to discount her. And from that instant, we trust this most sensible of voices to incorporate both the irrational and our doubt about it. In doing so, she's invited us into the supernatural experiences so common to her.

She speculates a few paragraphs later about the auras of eye migraines that torment her—allowing neurological possibilities for her ghost-related experiences. Above all, we're convinced of her firm curiosity about her encounters with the supernatural, her willingness to explore any explanation for them.

So later when, as a child in a garden, she has a run-in with the ultimate evil—one could only call it demonic though she doesn't go that far—she doesn't have to disavow the reality of the event to accommodate our doubt. The voice has made room for us before. Mantel needs only stick to physical facts and her child's reaction:

> The faintest movement, a ripple, a disturbance of
> the air. I can sense a spiral, a lazy buzzing swirl, like
> flies; but it is not flies. There is nothing to see. There
> is nothing to smell. There is nothing to hear. But it is
> motion, its insolent shift, makes my stomach heave.
> I can sense—at the periphery, the limit of all my
> senses—the dimensions of the creature. It is as high as
> a child of two. Its depth is a foot, fifteen inches. The
> air stirs around it, invisibly. I am cold, and rinsed by
> nausea. I cannot move. I am shaking. . . . This is the
> beginning of shame.

Whether you doubt Mantel's "reality" in this passage, you can have no doubt that she's reporting something ineffably real to her. (A similar type of entity inhabits her novel *Beyond Black*, among the most overpoweringly disturbing books I know—on a par with *Turn of the Screw* or the best of Stephen King.)

So, too, must voice confess to readers any moral bankruptcy, as in Tobias Wolff's *This Boy's Life*:

> I was a liar. Even though I lived in a place where
> everyone knew who I was, I couldn't help but try
> to introduce new versions of myself as my interests
> changed, and as other versions of myself failed to
> persuade. I was also a thief.

What's so winning about this confession is the author's self-aware reason for it: he's trying to forge a self, and when popular opinion interferes with the process, Wolff fabricates to fool his audience and further what he sees as self-reshaping. It's the gift of self-awareness: who hasn't wanted to be somebody different and tried to scudge the public into buying the act? Rather than ruining the reader's confidence in the author's pages, the confession actually bolsters her belief. We can accept anything from a memoirist but deceit, which is—almost always—a shallow person's lack of self-knowledge.

Even somebody I might not otherwise care for can compel my attention when speaking out of hard-felt experience and self-knowledge. On airplanes, we've all been stranded next to some chatty, perfectly nice but duller-than-a-rubber-knife human being, and we've all faked sleep to escape that chatter. Yet when travelers' anonymity permits said bore to speak out of some profoundly felt experience, I often find myself riveted by the confessions of somebody I'd otherwise dread spending even a five-minute elevator ride with. That person's living, breathing inner expression, which (when told with heart and candor) includes some parcels of radical suffering and joy . . . well, it always captures me.

For speaking from passionately felt events is risky. Emotional stakes make drama, which is a conflict with feeling and danger mysteriously contained in a human body's small space.

Don't get me wrong—a writer's voice doesn't have to be effusive or operatic to work. Nobody's more reticent than Conroy or Nabokov, say. But no one doubts the depths of their feeling, however cool their overall tones.

As often as I've been bored by a shallow seat partner fronting some fake self, I've been transfixed by watching lived passion radiate off a stranger's face. Even the most buttoned-up or recalcitrant person, trying to restrain feeling, can't help but convey it in close proximity if she's telling those core stories that've seemingly shaped who she is. The least articulate of confessors can—in fleeting moments of connection—move me as a great symphony does. And it's from the need to capture the shared connections between us that symphonies were invented. Ditto memoirs.

All drama depends on our need to connect with one another. And we're all doomed to drama; even the most privileged among us suffer the torments of the damned just going about the business of being human. People we adore drop dead or die over tortured years. We're born ugly and poor, or rich and handsome but uncared-for. In even the best families, loved ones—however inadvertently—manage to destroy each other's hope. They fail to show up at the key instant, or they show up serving grief and shame when tenderness is starved for.

One great side effect of my own work is how often strangers skip the small talk to confide the more turbulent patches of their lives. It's an odd phenomenon that I have never not been moved by such a tale. And I'm not that compassionate or generous, either.

Still, a living, breathing human being—even a boneheaded

or barely articulate one—conveys so much in person. The physical fact of a creature with heart thrumming and neurons flickering—what Shakespeare called the "poor, bare, forked animal"—compels us all; we're all hardwired in moments of empathy to see ourselves in another. Hearing each other's stories actually raises our levels of the feel-good hormone oxytocin, which is what nursing mothers secrete when they breastfeed—what partly helps them bond with their young. It helps to join us together in some tribal way.

It's harder to translate lived experience onto a page. A story told poorly is life made small by words. The key details are missing, and the sentences might have been spoken by anybody. We need a special verbal device to unpack all that's hidden in the writer's heart so we can freshly relive it: a voice.

Unfortunately, nobody tells a writer how hard cobbling together a voice is. Look under "voice" in a writing textbook, and they talk about things that seem mechanical—tone, diction, syntax. *Doh*, the writer says with a forehead smack. Diction is merely word choice, what variety of vocabulary you favor. Syntax is whether sentences are long or short, how they're shaped, with or without dependent clauses, etc. Some sentences meander, others fire off like machine-gun runs. Tone is the emotional tenor of the sentences; it's how the narrator feels about the subject. Robert Frost said anytime he heard wordless voices through a wall, tone told him who was angry, who bemused, who about to cry. For me psyche equals voice, so your own psyche—how you think and see and wonder and scudge and suffer—also determines such factors as pacing and what you write about when. Since all such literary decisions for a memoirist are offshoots of character, I often find that any bafflement I face on the page about these factors is instantly answered once I find the right voice.

In Frank Conroy's *Stop-Time* (1967) he doesn't try to jack up a mediocre experience into dramatic spectacle. Rather, he takes a small moment and renders it so poetically you can't forget it. Here he's a way-smart, pseudo-delinquent high school student before school.

> Eyes closed, head back, I drank directly from the carton of milk, taking long gulps while cold air from the refrigerator spilled out onto my bare feet. Leaving an inch for [my stepfather's] coffee, I replaced the carton and pushed the fat door shut. End of breakfast.

The scene captures the feral hunger of any adolescent male standing in the fridge door. Yet it *feels* so specific—the long gulps, the cold spilling on his feet, even the inch of milk he has to leave behind for his stepfather. Is he doing it thoughtfully or sullenly or automatically? You'll have to read the book to find out, for Conroy manages to make even the most quotidian event *mean*. Nobody's rendered a teen's cynical morning haste any better. And the rhythm of the paragraph: the long sentence—three lines—followed by a short sentence—two—leads up to three perfunctory words "End of breakfast." This is an outlaw boy scrabbling for small sustenance, and the authority of the fat fridge door and his seminal voice—in the context of the rest of the book—lines up with Conroy's cool, I-can-take-being-neglected persona. So powerful is Conroy's voice that—at the zenith of his powers—he's able to sexualize the throwing of a yoyo:

> That it was vaguely masturbatory seems inescapable.
> I doubt that half the pubescent boys in America
> could have been captured by any other means. . . .
> A single Loop-the-Loop might represent, in some
> mysterious way, the act of masturbation, but to break
> down the entire repertoire into the three stages of
> throw, trick, and return representing erection, climax,
> and detumescence seems immoderate.

Conroy puts himself into a trance practicing the yoyo, thus disassociating from his family's profound lack of care. Finding that "cool" spot—in the old hep-cat jazz sense of finding a groove—means finding order, silence, a place where time can stop. In such instants of cool, the boy-in-pain Conroy can vanish. He'll later find sex and music and liquor and driving too fast as other modes of escape into selfless silence.

Having taught Conroy's *Stop-Time* for some thirty years, I can testify that students seem to trust this voice. They believe it—that it won't lie or mislead, fabricate events or pander, confess the lesser sin to hide the greater, bore or beg for pity. Ergo, in literary terms, it sounds true.

Again: voice grows from the nature of a writer's talent, which stems from innate character. Just as a memoirist's nature bestows her magic powers on the page, we also wind up seeing how selfish or mean-spirited or divisive she is or was. We don't see events objectively; we perceive them through ourselves. And we remember through a filter of both who we are now and who we once were.

So the best voices include a writer's insides. Watching her mind feel around to concoct or figure out events, you never lose sight of the ego's shape, its blind spots, dislikes, wants. The books I reread don't seek to record as film does—a visual medium tethered to surface action (these days, in popular film, the flashier the better); nor as a history does—by weighing and measuring various sources and crafting a balanced perspective.

To tell the truth, such a memoirist can't help but show at each bump in the road how her perceptual filter is distorting what's being taken in. In other words, she questions her own perceptions as part of the writing process. The deeper—and, ergo, more plausible-sounding—writer inquires.

Just as memory distorts, so too does the ego's synthesizer shape even the simplest of our sensations, and voice should reflect that distortion. Conroy in his no-nonsense milk guzzling doesn't sound frail or sentimental, nor does Wright in his righteous rage. The noise each makes speaks his character into being. Both sound tough and cynical, even as kids. Since a personal theory about the world and one's place in it can make it appear so, we can assume they're as wary in the world as on the page. They translate events coming at them to conform to ideas about how they presume stuff works—in their cases perhaps through a scrim of smart, canny suspicion.

But how dare I speak of truth in memoir, when it's common knowledge that the subjective, egoistic perception is a priori warped by falsehood—perhaps mildly so in self-serving desires, or wildly so in hardwired paranoia? A Buddhist monk might call how the ego takes in the world *maya* or "delusion"; a psychologist might point out how you project past traumas onto today's innocent events. So how's veracity possible?

It's not that memories aren't shady, but the self-aware memoirist constantly pokes and prods at his doubts like a tongue on a black tooth. The trick to fashioning a deeper, truer voice involves understanding how you might misperceive as you go along; thus looking at things more than one way. The goal of a voice is to speak not with objective authority but with subjective curiosity.

For me, say, a penchant for gloom has to be confessed to throughout any book I write. Bleak humor right at the edge of being wrong has kept me alive, so it's wound up in my work. Asked by my sister why I was sexually assaulted as a child but she wasn't, I quipped, "Maybe you're not cute enough"—which takes one of the darkest events in my life and tries to turn it into a putdown for somebody else. Talk about grim. To chirp my story like some bouncy cheerleader would be to lie. That grimness has to make it in.

A believable voice notes how the self may or may not be inventing reality, morphing one's separate "truths." Most of us don't read the landscape so much as we beam it from our eyeballs.

The inability to don angel wings—to shirk culpability or justify past sins—seems innate to the voice of every memoirist I revere. The life chroniclers who endure as real artists come across as folks particularly schooled in their own rich inner geographies. A quest for self-knowledge drives such a writer to push past the normal vanity she brings to party dressing. She somehow manages to show up at the ball boldly naked.

A memoirist's nature—the self who shapes memory's filter—will prove the source of her talent. By talent, I mean not just surface literary gifts, though those are part of the package, but life experience, personal values, approach, thought processes, perceptions, and innate character.

Here's Elif Batuman in *The Possessed: Adventures with Russian Books and the People Who Read Them*, dramatizing her talent for surreal metaphor along with her passion for Russian lit. The passage comes from her magnificently slapstick chapter detailing an academic conference on Batuman's hero, Soviet martyr Isaac Babel.

> When the Russian Academy of Sciences puts together an author's *Collected Works*, they aren't aiming for something you can put in a suitcase and run away with. The "millennium" edition of Tolstoy fills a hundred volumes and weighs as much as a newborn beluga whale. (I brought my bathroom scale to the library and weighed it, ten volumes at a time.)

The detail of her hauling a scale to the library marks her an adorably obsessive kook, and we hope her passion for Russian lit will infect us. (Hint: it does.)

Like Batuman's work, Babel's is also earmarked by shocking juxtapositions and unforgettable similes. One of his *Red Cavalry* stories begins, "The orange sun is rolling across the sky like a severed head."

You can watch Batuman hone her talent for metaphor if you read the first version of this essay, as I did, in the literary cult mag *n+1*, where Tolstoy's collected volumes first weighed as much as "a large timber wolf." Most of us would've let the wolf metaphor stand—it's jolting and funny and echoes a Russian landscape. But she rewrote, and the beluga whale is the far better animal, springing as it does from salty caviar, which echoes the lost empire of the czars. Plus the whale, like Tolstoy, is a behemoth, reigning in a rarer element than the wolf. It's hard even to believe he's a mammal like the rest of us.

As you start out in rough drafts, setting down stories as clearly as you can, there begins to burble up onto the page what's exclusively yours both as a writer and a human being. If you trust the truth enough to keep unveiling yourself on the page—no matter how shameful those revelations may at first seem—the book will naturally structure itself to maximize what you're best at. You're best at it because it sits at the core of your passions.

Cheryl Strayed, whose *Wild* still rides the best-seller list, was blessed with a passion for poetry that informed her language. That and the discipline to keep a daily journal during her solo hike of the Pacific Trail gave her the skeleton of that book. Strayed speaks of truth as a quest: "I tell students they want to find the true, truer, truest story." Her first draft scraped the surface, but she found deeper psychological truths in revisions. How you approach the truth depends on your passions—Russian books and surreal metaphor, journal keeping and poetry and hiking.

You can witness two different talents approaching some of the same material by reading brothers Geoffrey and Tobias Wolff. Geoffrey's seminal *Duke of Deception* (1979) partly grew from his extraordinary skills as a biographer: he used a historian's investigative research to rout out his con-man father's lies. Research and interviewing were gifts Geoffrey had mastered in his fascinating and immaculately documented biography of Lost Generation suicide Harry Crosby, *Black Sun*. Geoffrey's memoir uses photos and documents to announce it as an investigated work. But nonfiction's notions of the truth kept evolving. By the time his brother Tobias brought out *This Boy's Life* in 1989, he used no photos, no interviews. His work is an act of memory. Two men, two talents, two approaches.

Developing a voice is actually learning how to lodge your own memories inside someone else's head. In some ways the narrator comes to exist as a stand-in for the reader.

$$\cdot \ \cdot \ \cdot$$

The only way I know to develop a voice is to write your way into one. As a memoirist moves words around on a page, telling stories, she starts to uncover that thing she does best, which should stay in view during most of the book.

And you need not be fancy in diction and syntax to win an audience—only true. Frank McCourt's *Angela's Ashes* uses the proletariat's blunt, monosyllabic diction to work magic.

> My father and mother should have stayed in New York where they met and married and where I was born. Instead, they returned to Ireland when I was four, my brother, Malachy, three, the twins, Oliver and Eugene, barely one, and my sister Margaret, dead and gone.
>
> When I look back on my childhood I wonder how I survived at all. It was, of course, a miserable childhood: the happy childhood is hardly worth your while. Worse than the ordinary miserable childhood is the miserable Irish childhood, and worse yet is the miserable Irish Catholic childhood.
>
> People everywhere brag and whimper about the woes of their early years, but nothing can compare with the Irish version: the poverty; the shiftless loquacious alcoholic father; the pious defeated mother moaning by the fire; pompous priests; bullying schoolmasters; the English and the terrible things they did to us for eight hundred long years.
>
> Above all—we were wet.

Other than a peppering of Latinate words like *loquacious*, McCourt uses words we learned by fifth grade. It's *what* he writes and *when* and the directness of his utterance that we connect with. A polymath like Nabokov (more on him in the next chapter) wows us with his linguistic surface; McCourt works to make us identify with him more.

The first paragraph posits family trouble—*My father and mother should have stayed in New York*—then draws the simplest list of siblings, ending with the awful presence of a dead infant. And since McCourt knows in some ways that we as readers fear the cliché of an awful Irish childhood, he addresses that fear right off. So he comes straight to where the reader's cynicism about his enterprise hides. McCourt then routs it out with mockery: *the pious defeated mother moaning by the fire; pompous priests, bullying schoolmasters. . . .* He ends with a simple, understated, carnal joke on himself in the physical cold of his island home: "Above all—we were wet." McCourt raised psychological states while wowing us with both tragedy and humor—promises for what the book will hold.

He would've failed trying to use Nabokov's diction, syntax, or psychological approach.

5 | Don't Try This at Home: The Seductive, Narcissistic Count

> . . . *I mean what*
> *would you do if you had to create Beauty?*
> *I'm afraid I'd start screaming, the most irksome*
> *forms of insects coming from my mouth. I'm afraid*
> *I'd come up with Death.*
>
> Dean Young, "One Story"

So enchanting is the atmosphere Nabokov conjures in my brain that reading him almost rewires it. I lift my face from a folded-down page to find colors brighter, edges sharper. Trash I glimpse on my otherwise shoddy street—a ticket stub or lipsticky cigarette butt—come across as souvenirs from some intrigue that dissolved right before I looked up. The world becomes a magic collage or mysterious art box à la found-object assembler Joseph Cornell. And it works every time you reread—a miraculous widget for perceptual transformation. As Philip Larkin once said of poetry's slot machine, you put the penny of your attention into it, pull a handle, and a feeling comes out. Like my students, I've tried to copy Nabokov's mysterious dance methods, and I looked like a fool—some stout and hirsute cross-dresser trying to pass as pretty in pink ballerina tights.

Having taught this book at least a dozen times, I still find it a mystery. Trying to catalogue Nabokov's talents would take a library, and yet not to call out *Speak, Memory* in a book about memoir would be like Fourth of July sans fireworks.

Looked at through the lens of a more ordinary writer's gifts, *Speak, Memory* leaves out much that a normal reader tends to identify with. Yet we wander its pages with wonder and feel bereft as any exile at its end.

Recently, from sheer frustration, I started combing it for what *isn't* there, which—it surprised me to find—is the kind of deep link with an author that hooks me into most other great memoirs. *Speak, Memory* lacks long-run, personally dramatic stories of the type we associate with normal plots. There's no dialogue; the occasional instant or anecdote, but very few scenes. You're intimate with the writer's thought processes without feeling he has anything in common with the likes of you. The writing is intoxicating and irresistible—but you can't find your experience anywhere in it. His extreme refinement frees him from the humdrum where most of us live. Novelist Jenny Offill refers to him as "an art monster": "Nabokov didn't even fold his own umbrella. [His wife] licked his stamps for him."

The creature you find in *Speak, Memory* is rare enough to be zoo-worthy. He's not just smarter but somehow more effete than most of us without seeming put on. Resenting him for it would be like resenting a gazelle for her grace. He doesn't sound prissy painting himself as a cultivated synesthete who can hear colors and see music, nor vain talking as a polyglot who translates his own work back and forth into many languages. He's just your standard virtuoso aristocrat from a gilded age.

Which is the miracle of his talent. He has shaped the book to highlight his own magnificent way of viewing the world, a viewpoint that so eats your head that you never really leave his very oddly bejeweled skull, and you value things in the book's context as he does, never missing what you otherwise adore in another kind of writer.

In fact, if you could list some of the information Nabokov reports about his relationships apart from his magical atmosphere, you'd find he fails to meet many measures we use for being a halfway decent person. If we weren't so in love with him, we might cringe from him. His aristocratic social mores and emotional quirks—absent the beguiling atmosphere he woos us into—could come off as foppish at best or malignantly misanthropic at worst.

The book is a mesmerizing meditation on the nature of beauty, time, and loss, played out against backdrops of fairy-dusted interiors. And it's a cry of longing for his lost parents and of joy for his wife and son. Nabokov unabashedly identifies with imperial Russia's lush allure as the rich lived it in the early 1900s—enchanted rooms he steers us through page after page. He gives us philosophy and moments of transcendence. He leaps and drags us in his wake across the century, and we follow him without envy at his privilege. We're just glad to get past the velvet rope.

Nothing in his existence is banal. He is never bored or irritated. His parents are never less than glorious dolls, incapable of doing anything petty or commonplace. Both "shone like the sun." His mother wears white and shades of rose, bestowing on him sugary advice, i.e., love with all your soul and leave the rest to fate. His father, resplendent in Horse Guard uniform, "with that smooth golden swell of cuirass burning upon his chest and back," is the luminous king in a myth. Nabokov gets away with this by making us fall in love with his aristocratic mindscape.

Of all his talents, it's Nabokov's flair for carnality—by which, again, I mean physicality, not sexuality—that first lures me in. He can light on a physical object and—by filtering it through his perceptual machine—transform it into a relic that shoots off poetic associations like sparks. His whole childhood seems devoted to ingesting as much beauty from memory as he can wolf down—thus forging the lost empire into art before it turns to ash in his memory. He makes these objects signify in metaphorical ways that merge them with the book's themes: he must, as an expression of love for the lost, become sophisticated enough in taste to travel back and forth through time at will, to find the underlying patterns that order what's otherwise been obliterated. The whole effort is a salvage operation with life-or-death stakes, and the "plot"—so far as one exists—organizes itself around his making a sensibility fine enough to save the "perceptual Eden" he claims he was born into.

In another writer's hands, to focus on a single object at length reads as off-point or decorative. But for Nabokov, every object portends a whole slew of other meanings—ideological, moral, spiritual—that weave into the book's leitmotifs.

So the objects he dwells on aren't just pretty gewgaws from antique parlors; he infuses them with emotional consequence and symbolic weight and philosophical resonance. Early on, he starts training you to read into things like a necromancer deciphering the stars.

He's a kid in a cot making a tent of his bedclothes, "shadowy snowslides of linen," and that crib exists for me as though I'd wallowed in it. And it's his mother's jewels he played with in the crib—rings and tiaras and so forth:

> [A] certain beautiful, delightfully solid garnet-dark crystal egg left over from some forgotten Easter; I used to chew a corner of the bedsheet until it was thoroughly soaked and then wrap the egg in it so tightly, so as to admire and re-lick the warm, ruddy glitter of the snugly enveloped facets that came seeping through with a miraculous completeness of glow and color.

A lesser writer might sound florid detailing an object's jewel-like hue with phrases like "miraculous completeness." But in Nabokov's case, his dramatic devouring of the egg enacts his actual physical passion for splendor while granting the object psychological power. He calls sucking on it "not yet the closest I got to feeding on beauty."

So that egg is stone-cold food, only nurturing to the poetic mind, which is the altar at which Nabokov worships. The fake egg is maternal and primordial, and it holds in its ruby light birth's promise—and he, the artist-to-be, is nursing on it. This is baby Nabokov, the nascent connoisseur coming to consciousness before his mysterious, radiant god—timeless beauty. That stone garnet egg is cold and indestructible, but somehow mother's milk for him.

This description comes early enough to help establish in a reader's mind the poetic resonance of objects as part of the book's inner struggle. Siphoning up beauty isn't only a leitmotif; it's a form of survival.

So he can devote a chapter to butterfly hunting, while his father being shot in exile occupies less than a moment, and the two events in no way seem off balance in the writer's account books. Of course, it's his father who taught him to stalk through the fields with a net, so in some way the folded, papery insects are paternal heirlooms, short-lived flying flowers—sacred icons from the divine patriarch known for his cutlass and boxed dueling pistols.

The whole Russian revolution that ruined his family in every sense is mere background music to Nabokov's refinement. It will take a keen eye and keener taste and the keenest of philosophical minds to rescue his lost beloveds from the ravages of time, and it's his inability to control time externally—to resurrect them—that serves as his inner enemy. In a great memoir, some aspect of the writer's struggle for self often serves as the book's organizing principle, and the narrator's battle to become whole rages over the book's trajectory. So being an aficionado of beauty and philosophy makes Nabokov's parents "alive" for him in the book. In this way, developing his aesthetic sensibility becomes a life-or-death matter, not a peacock's vain preening.

Part of his singular skill—manifested in his voice—is translating philosophical ideas into physical or carnal metaphors; in this way he is not unlike Babel and Batuman. He'll somehow smoosh ideas into unforgettable images. Instead of saying, as I might, dully enough, "The whole universe is small compared to a single memory," Nabokov injects feeling into the idea—and makes it syntactically memorable as hell—by conjuring his own wonder with an image we'll find wonderful ourselves.

How small the cosmos (a kangaroo's pouch would
hold it), how paltry and puny in comparison to human
consciousness, to a single individual recollection, and its
expression in words!

Like any master writer, he's found the "trick" of doing what
he most excels at: structuring the voice so that his talent sits in
the foreground.

Students love trying to imitate Nabokov, which teaches them
a lot—mostly about why not to imitate somebody wired so differently from yourself. Nabokov wannabes don't sound just
like turds, but like pretentious turds. The writer's best voice
will grow from embracing her own "you-ness"—which I call
talent, and which is best expressed in voice.

Which brings me back to that simplest of voice building
blocks: diction. Nabokov uses a diction more ornate than would
fit most of us. For the vast majority of writers, we're better off
with simpler vocabulary—the shorter, often monosyllabic words
you use all the dang time. Unless you're like my friend, poet
Brooks Haxton (who translates Greek, Latin, French, Hebrew,
and German), throwing in three-dollar words will just make you
look like a dick. So you're better off writing *fuck* than *copulate*—
the first has Germanic origins, the second derives from Latinate
language. There are no rules, but Germanic words tend to be
thought of as "low." It's the vocabulary of the street, of childhood or the underprivileged. The other vocabulary is often seen
as "high"—the parlance of science and diplomacy. In France
there was an actual academy that screened out words deemed

too shitty (Germanic) or scrofulous (Latinate) to join their fancy dictionary.

Nabokov's sentences go on for lines and sometimes pages, and his highfalutin diction sprouts naturally from his polyglot education and rarefied background.

His psychological need, stated early in the book, is to be free of time, which will eradicate the past he's trying to hold on to—he almost can't believe, we sometimes think, that his mind can't change the facts. So being untethered by chronology becomes—like his constant trolling for beauty—part of the book's driving engine, almost working like a plot. He opens with the subject:

> The cradle rocks above an abyss, and common sense tells us that our existence is but a brief crack of light between two eternities of darkness. . . . I rebel against this state of affairs. I feel the urge to take my rebellion outside and picket nature.

Throughout the book, he talks about how "the walls of time separate me and my bruised fists from the free world of timelessness." Later he writes, "Initially, I was unaware that time, so boundless at first blush, was a prison."

What caps off time for us, of course, is death. Nabokov loves "twinning"—finding matching patterns in disparate places and laying them together like butterfly wings. The cradle that opens the book becomes—by the first chapter's end—a coffin, presumably his father's.

He ends the chapter with that coffin in a long, unspooling-for-yards sentence that starts with a memory from young Nabokov's childhood place at the table. He watches his exalted father perform what he calls "an act of levitation," when peasants toss him in the air three times in "the mighty heave-ho"—their way of cheering the landowner lord for some gift. He flies up and hangs suspended in the window as if by magic. The subsequent metaphor takes us on a long journey.

> And then there he would be, on his last and loftiest flight, reclining, as if for good, against the cobalt blue of the summer noon, like one of those paradisiac personages who comfortably soar, with such a wealth of folds on their garments, on the vaulted ceiling of a church while below, one by one, the wax tapers in mortal hands light up to make a swarm of minute flames in the mist of incense, and the priest chants of eternal repose, and funeral lilies conceal the face of whoever lies there, among the swimming lights, in the open coffin.

Ezra Pound said rhythm in poetry is "cutting a form in time." Nabokov's form in this chapter—the cradle at its opening, the coffin at its end—makes a satisfying little click in the reader's head. The shape of it works to satisfy you like repetition and variation in music.

Now I'm not naive enough to think every reader makes the conscious association between the two containers for a human, "fore and aft," as Nabokov calls it, baby/corpse. But such is my own faith in poetry, which taps into both the unconscious and memory, that I believe finding the coffin at chapter's end gives even the most reckless reader the sweet sense of some underlying order. I'm enough of a poetry fan to believe it can work like voodoo under a reader's awareness. Nabokov makes you drool like one of Pavlov's dogs for these moments when he takes one scene in time and stitches it to another.

And finding lost connections in these "clicking" or twinning moments becomes what you shop for as you read, thus providing momentum. From early on, each flight from time implies longing and a desperate scramble to reenter the past. So when he sails from one era to start what would (in another writer's book) be digressive, we gladly fly into another age with Nabokov—it becomes a forward movement, not a sideways detour.

> I confess I do not believe in time. I like to fold
> my magic carpet, after use, in such a way as to
> superimpose one part of the pattern upon another.
> Let visitors trip. And the highest enjoyment of
> timelessness . . . is when I stand among rare butterflies
> and their food plants. This is ecstasy, and behind the
> ecstasy is something else, which is hard to explain.
> It is like a momentary vacuum into which rushes all
> that I love. A sense of oneness with sun and stone.

"Oneness with sun and stone" sounds not unlike being God. And from his state of timelessness, he *is* a god at resurrecting the lost.

Another twinning example. At one point, he describes a boyhood encounter with General Kuropatkin, head of the Russian Army in the east, who lines up on a divan ten matches for young Vladimir to make a smooth ocean surface. When the general tips the matches up in pairs to look like sharp waves, that pattern represents a stormy sea. Fifteen years later, as Papa Nabokov flees the Bolsheviks across southern Russia, he meets what he presumes is a peasant in a sheepskin coat who asks for a light. Of course it's the old general, seeking a match. The twin moments are jammed together to reveal a great truth—how the powerful fall, the matches are burnt out and lost.

But as for the general himself, he's a pawn in the pattern, not a character we've been made to care about. "I hope that old Kuropatkin, in his rustic disguise, managed to evade Soviet imprisonment, *but that is not the point*" (emphasis mine).

In other words, whether this man lived or died interests the writer not nearly as much as his own poetic associations.

> What pleases me is the evolution of the match theme: those magic ones [Kuropatkin] had shown me had been trifled with and mislaid, and his armies had also vanished, and everything had fallen through, like my toy trains. . . . *The following of such thematic designs through one's life should be, I think, the true purpose of autobiography.* (Emphasis mine.)

Nabokov's not giving a crap about the general as a human critter would read as hideously hateful in any other writer's book, particularly one where the writer's warmth or heart sits at the core of her talent—Angelou, say, or McCourt. And Nabokov's beloveds are wholly vague except insofar as they're recipients of his exaltations. The characters he sketches in keenest detail tend to be people he scorns, which differs from what we expect from most writers. Mostly we like them to sound "fair." It's one thing for Tobias Wolff to snark at his tyrannical first stepfather with his *nyah nyah* note in *This Boy's Life*: "[He] used to say what I didn't know would fill a book. Well, here it is." But we may have thought less of Wolff as a narrator if he undertook the kind of grotesque portraits Nabokov can paint of family underlings like his neurasthenic governess Mademoiselle.

> Her hands were unpleasant because of the froggy gloss on their tight skin besprinkled with brown

> ecchymotic spots. . . . I think of her hands. Her
> trick of peeling rather than sharpening a pencil,
> the point held toward her stupendous and sterile
> bosom swathed in green wool. The way she had
> of inserting her little finger into one ear and
> vibrating it very rapidly. . . . Always panting a little,
> her mouth slightly open and emitting in quick
> succession a series of asthmatic puffs.

Any character in a teen movie exhibiting even one of these qualities would be doomed for two hours to no end of high school cruelty. In case we haven't judged her harshly enough from this portrait, at one point, he dubs her a creature without a soul—brutal.

And yet we don't recoil from him, because he's created a context where he's entitled to do this. For him to feign sympathy for her or to pose as a man of the people would come off as smarmy. The following of poetic themes can be the purpose for him, since that's the nature of his particular psyche and character and emotional patois and camber. Few of us have such philosophical natures so attached to deep emotional places, nor the effete sensibility for such pattern-making or thematic explorations (maybe Hong Kingston in *The Woman Warrior*).

Nabokov's not cold—few books are more passionate. He can make you tear up as he mourns his family: "[Beings] that I had most loved in the security of my childhood had been turned to ashes or shot through the heart." His outbursts for his loved ones pepper the book, but love is often manifest in a more oddly abstract form than most writers would be able to pull off.

> Whenever I start thinking of my love for a person, I
> am in the habit of immediately drawing radii from

my love—from my heart, from the tender nucleus of
a personal matter—to monstrously remote points in
the universe. Something impels me to measure the
consciousness of my love against such unimaginable
and incalculable things as the behavior of nebulae.

When most of us think of our love for a person, we think
of the actual *person*. So a normal writer, drifting into this kind
of metaphor in the midst of her memoir, would sound like a
literary show-off avoiding the point. Because Nabokov's mind
naturally moves in a metaphorical direction, he's trained us
to read these excursions as emotional events tethered to the
writer's survival.

He devotes way more time to falling in love with poetry
than he does to either brother. Yet we barely notice his completely ignoring one brother* and barely mentioning the other,
Sergey, who was probably gay, based on what Vladimir read in
a teen diary, which he showed—rather cruelly—to a tutor. Yet
the brothers are ten months apart, and as kids, Vladimir admits
to being both "the coddled one" and "something of a bully."
We accept that situation as part of the universe we've begun
to inhabit: "[Sergey] is the mere shadow in the background
of my richest recollections." The two brothers cross paths in
Cambridge, where Sergey's dismissed as a crap tennis player;
and in Paris, where he sometimes "dropped by for a chat."
Nabokov loses sight of him during the war—how is it possible
this isn't a bigger deal to the writer? I wonder. He later learns
that Sergey died in a concentration camp. Nabokov's cagey explanation for this brother's absence fills one vague sentence:

* (In the index, he appears as Nabokov, Krill: 49, 256-257)

"For some reason, I find it inordinately hard to speak about my brother." Then the reader hops over this guy's corpse as glibly as Nabokov seems to; on we go to the next ravishing scene.

Still, using devices more common to other memoirists, Nabokov can draw tears from me at certain passages as predictably as if turned on by a spigot. Students who fear sentimentality as death have to study Nabokov, who proves that sentimentality is only emotion you haven't proven to the reader—emotion without vivid evidence. For Nabokov, memory itself is a country, and his tender reflections, coupled with longing, move us even more perhaps in coming from a speaker who can be so cool.

> I see again my schoolroom in Vyra, the blue roses
> on the wallpaper, the open window. Its reflection
> fills the mirror above the leathern couch where my
> uncle sits, gloating over a tattered book. A sense of
> security, of well-being, of summer warmth, pervades
> my memory. That robust reality makes a ghost of
> the present. The mirror brims with brightness: a
> bumblebee has entered the room and bumps against
> the ceiling. Everything is as it should be, nothing will
> ever change, nobody will ever die.

The above passage shows how an odd instant in time can endure in memory and reassemble itself decades later, the writer producing in the reader that very sense of security on the brink, which begins to tip and shiver toward desolation with that last phrase: "nobody will ever die."

Of course there are a thousand such more common moments uncommonly written in *Speak, Memory*, but mostly Nabokov structured the whole thing to play to his particular strengths—

twinning, metaphor, poetic moments of transcending time, carnal luxury. He found that talent for his talent. He sets us up early on to assign emotional value to his abilities. Once we understand his process, we can watch him frisk around like a rabbit, leaping forward and back in lengthy descriptions. He's imbued with emotional heft and meaning that very leaping, which would seem capricious or vain in another's work. The *process* of his thought has become the point of the book, form marrying into meaning as it does in poetry: a literary miracle.

6 | Sacred Carnality

My holy of holies is the human body.

Anton Chekhov, May 1888

Carnality sits at the root of the show-don't-tell edict that every writing teacher harps on all the time, because it works. By *carnal*, I mean, Can you apprehend it through the five senses? In writing a scene, you must help the reader employ smell and taste and touch as well as image and noise. The more carnal a writer's nature, the better she'll be at this, and there are subcategories according to the senses. A great glutton can evoke the salty bite of pastrami on black rye; the sex addict will excel at smooth flesh; the one with a painterly eye visual beauty, etc. Every memoir should brim over with the physical experiences that once streamed in—the smell of garlicky gumbo, your hand in an animal's fur, the ocean's phosphor lighting up bodies underwater all acid green. Of all memoir's five elements, carnality is the most primary and necessary and—luckily for me as a teacher—the most easy to master.

My Texas oil-worker daddy introduced me as a kid to the raconteur's need for physical evidence when he told me a story about selling fake moonshine to some city boys. His brother was driving off with Daddy hanging on the running board of a Model T when a pursuer driving alongside snatched Daddy's pants off from behind.

Bull dookey, I said. You saw that in *Bugs Bunny*.

"You don't believe me?" I didn't. "I had this shirt on when it happened."

My mouth slung itself open.

It's sad how long I believed stories based on arbitrary physical objects that my daddy fished out from his past and plunked down into my present, like that shirt. It became totemic evidence that elevated the tall tale into reality.

Getting sophisticated about carnal writing means selecting sensual data—items, odors, sounds—to recount details based on their psychological effects on a reader. A great detail feels particular in a way that argues for its truth. A reader can take it in. The best have extra poetic meaning. In some magic way, the detail from its singular position in a room can help to evoke the rest of the whole scene, the way Conroy doing pages on the yo-yo evokes his body kinesthetically in the instant.

The great writer trolls the world for totemic objects to place on a page. In every genre, it's key.

Playwright and short-story genius Anton Chekhov could hypodermically inject an item so iconographic, so reverberant with meaning, that its presence almost recounts a whole character. In his seminal "Lady with a Dog," a rake at a summer holiday resort seduces a pious young wife over a period of weeks, and afterward, as she sobs in bed, he cuts a slice of watermelon. The butchered fruit isn't a symbolic stand-in for the ruined woman, but the coolness of his appetite for it as she sobs speaks volumes. When one of the first confessional poets,

Robert Lowell, wants to describe the psychological state of his mother's tense, aristocratic home, he claims her claw-foot furniture has "an on tiptoe air," in the process making the cool Waspy atmosphere into a kind of character.

The first memoirist to lure me into her physical universe with that kind of exactitude may have been Maya Angelou in *I Know Why the Caged Bird Sings*. Standing before her church congregation on Easter, the child Angelou forgets her lines and feels caged inside a lavender taffeta dress she'd once thought was going to transform her into one of the "sweet little white girls who were everybody's dream of what was right with the world." That beloved white girl-ness—so at odds with the physical fact of herself—undercut any confidence she might have had. (Which partly comprises that inner enemy I'll talk about more soon.) As she squirms and puffs, scrambling inside to remember, the hand-me-down dress's silk rustles around her, sounding like "crepe paper on the back of hearses," this wonderful sonic metaphor evocative of a time and place when horse-drawn hearses were draped in that rivery fabric. Almost every one of Angelou's phrases in that initial scene possesses a kinesthetic element, so that we inhabit the girl's body, which she wears with shame.

Beginning with the sunshine, Angelou puts us in a place and time only she can report on:

> But Easter's early morning sun had shown the dress
> to be a plain ugly cut-down from a white woman's
> once-was-purple throwaway. It was old-lady-long
> too, but it didn't hide my skinny legs, which had been
> greased with Blue Seal Vaseline and powdered with
> Arkansas red clay. The age-faded color made my skin
> look dirty.

Her hyphenated adjectives—*once-was-purple, age-faded, old-lady-long*—capture the peculiar language of southern complaint. (*You no-tits-having* was an actual invective hurled around my East Texas neighborhood.) The detail of her bony legs covered with Vaseline and clay—a southern black alternative to stockings I first learned of from her—is singular to her time. No detail is Brand X or generic. It all springs, as Keats once said of metaphor, like leaves from a tree.

And Angelou's descriptions never flag as her soft-focus fantasy ends, so she's transformed into a too-big girl with hair "a kinky mass," also squinty eyes—"my daddy must've been a Chinaman." She's a girl "forced to eat pigs' tails and snouts." Further she has broad feet and "a space between her teeth that would hold a number-two pencil"—the tooth space even conjuring a kid's move of fitting a pencil there.

Think of all the dreadful carnal clichés Angelou might have chosen (other than *nappy*, which she does use once), and you twig to her talent for placing our bodies alive in a scene.

Strangely, readers "believe" what's rendered with physical clarity. I once had a reader say, "I knew when you put in that old can of Babbo cleanser you were telling the God's honest truth." A guy I played a kissing game with in junior high was stunned that thirty years later, I evoked his red shirt with a tiny sea horse embroidered on front. "You're some kinda witch if you remember that," he said.

Again, in instants of hyperarousal, focus narrows; sense memories from these states may sometimes stay brighter in recollection than others. Anybody juiced on adrenaline and the stress hormone cortisol—not unlike Angelou being scared in front of the church—registers sense impressions more intensely than in more typical time. Going back to the aforementioned kissing game, I can still distinctly feel myself inside the curved arms of the boy I'd so long had a crush on. Almost forty years later, I can still smell his Juicy Fruit gum. I put my hands up, almost to protect myself from standing too close, and my fingertips had the sea-horse outline imprinted on them.

Of course, physical details, however convincing, actually prove zip in terms of truth. Surely I misremember all kinds of stuff. Maybe the boy I kissed was chewing Bazooka Joe or Dubble Bubble, say. But I think in this case the specific memory—even if wrong—is permissible, because readers understand the flaws of memory and allow for them.

Noncarnal people may have to stretch to become memorable describers. We all start off sketching a character lightly—hair and eyes and weight like a driver's license—and a less thoughtful writer may fail to sully the page with that person's physical presence again, as if such a generic memory blurt makes an eternal impression. (As a kid, I was so revved up and anxious and hyper-vigilant that I studied people as if with a magnifying glass. Stimuli others barely register can still come across very loud to me.)

A haunting sense of place should ripple off any good memoir once the cover's closed, and you may reopen the front again as you would a gate to another land. Anybody with crisp recall can get half decent at describing stuff with practice. Hilary Mantel explains her own confidence in her memories as growing from their vivid physicality: "Though my early memories are patchy, I think they are not, or not entirely confabulation, and I believe this because of their overwhelming sensory power; they come complete, not like the groping, generalized formulations of the subjects fooled by the photograph. As I say 'I tasted,' I taste, and as I say 'I heard,' I hear; I am not talking about a Proustian moment, but a Proustian cine-film."

As they do for Mantel, the sharpest memories often give me the spooky sense of looking out from former eyeholes at a landscape decades-since gone. The old self comes back, the former face. When that transformation happens inside me, it's almost like I only have to set down what I see.

Compare two master writers—one in a noncarnal instant, the other in a carnal one. A passage from Robert Graves's 1929 *Good-Bye to All That*—while good as prose—tells more than shows us his psychic state after World War I: "I was still mentally and nervously organized for war. Shells used to come bursting on my bed at night, even though Nancy shared it with me; strangers in daytime would assume the faces of friends who had been killed. . . . I could not use a telephone, I felt sick every time I travelled by train, and to see more than two new people in a single day prevented me from sleeping."*

Don't mistake my view of Graves: he's an extremely carnal writer, and his scenes of trench warfare clench at a reader's bowels. But here the sentences have the quality more of a *semantic* memory than an *episodic* one—memory told more than memory lived. There is not a single scene but several condensed into phrases. He tells you he's sick but doesn't occupy the sick body. The only sense memory—large but not dwelled on above—is that of shells bursting in bed. Because they are

---

* Graves also notes that the flashbacks that haunted him for more than ten years all came from his first four months in France only. "The emotion-recording apparatus seems to have failed after Loos," he wrote; his memory sort of tanked up and stopped saving what passed before his eyes.

plural, the faces are less vivid to us. (Again, he saw plenty of ghosts in singular form—I'm only making a point.)

Compare this to the physical detail of Michael Herr's own "bad flash" in *Dispatches* (1977), which he likens to an old acid trip.

> Certain rock and roll would come in mixed with rapid fire and men screaming. Sitting over a steak in Saigon once I made nasty meat connections, rot and burning from the winter before in Hue. Worst of all, you'd see people walking around whom you'd watched die in aid stations and helicopters. The boy with the huge Adam's apple and the wire-rimmed glasses sitting by himself at a table on the Continental terrace had seemed much more nonchalant as a dead marine two weeks before.

Herr at first nearly faints, then does a double take and notes that the dead boy is not a ghost. The flashback seems triggered by smell, with "nasty meat connections" and "rot and burning."

Unlike Graves's plural flashbacks of "lost friends," Herr sees a particular ghost marine "with the huge Adam's apple and the wire-rimmed glasses." Herr goes on to describe his stress reaction in a way we as readers can enter: "My breath was gummed up in my throat and my face was cold and white, shake shake shake." (That wry *shake shake shake* is some of the rock-and-roll-speak that fuels the voice's engine in *Dispatches* and steers the reader away from pity, which he adroitly deflects with lyrics and dark humor.)

Carnal memories don't have to be traumatic, of course. Simple ones stick because of repetition. A neurologist friend took his college-age daughter to a new chain restaurant spun off from the one they'd visited every Saturday for a pumpkin muffin when she was a toddler. At the new place, my friend foisted a piece of his pumpkin muffin on his daughter without mentioning the old connection. From first bite, her eyes filled. She was remembering. She described every detail of the old place and how they'd go to the botanical garden after. "But it can't be right," she said, "because this place just opened."

You know in *Robocop* when Peter Weller gets molded into some kind of metal suit with computer eyes and clenchy, strongman hands? An excellent carnal writer fashions not a robot, but what feels like a breathing, tasting avatar the reader can climb inside, thus wearing the writer's hands and standing inside her shoes. The reader gets zipped into your skin.

7 | How to Choose a Detail

*Literature differs from life in that life is amorphously
full of detail, and rarely directs us toward it, whereas
literature teaches us to notice. Literature makes us
better noticers of life; we get to practice on life itself;
which in turn makes us better readers of detail in
literature; which in turn makes us better readers of life.*

James Wood, *How Fiction Works*

As a kid, one way I handled my own family crisis was to pick
on a littler kid next door, Mickey Heinz. Yes, I was picked on,
but I also did picking on back—part of the economy of misery
handed down from older to younger on the block. While writing *Liars' Club*, I interrogated my memory, coming up with
four possible details to give a reader.

1. A bunch of us dared him to take his pants off in his
   closet with a neighbor girl right before we knew his
   mama was coming home from a dash to the store.
2. I made him eat something nasty in a sandwich—
   mud or dogshit, I can't recall which.
3. I used to ask him to play hide-and-seek and then just
   go home while he looked all afternoon.

4. I got him to smoke Nestle's Quik rolled up in toilet
   paper, which blistered his tongue.

Number 1 would almost require a whole scene. It'd take
too long to tell. Plus the memory is mostly semantic—an idea
rather than concrete images. I didn't trust it. The story could
have been neighborhood legend. I had no physical visuals from
the story.

Number 2 also sounds like something I may have just heard.
Making somebody eat something awful in my neighborhood
was a common trick—maybe it wasn't this kid at all.

Number 3 isn't as dramatic as any of the other scenes.

But number 4, with the fake cigarette, is like nothing I've
heard elsewhere. It led to a string of physical details: i.e., one
dad across the street rolled his own smokes on a red-plastic-
and-tin roller. We snitched it from a kitchen drawer, along
with the Quik from a cabinet.

Those concrete images made me trust my memory of the
whole scene as mine, not just something I heard about. And
the carnality of the burned tongue is something anybody
who's ever sipped scalding coffee can practically feel. There's
an intimate "truth" that helps the reader enter the scene—
small and particular. I also remembered he showed his mother
the blistered tongue, and that we as a neighborhood listened
to his spanking in the bathroom after, which was also very
specific—"a hairbrush on his blubbery little ass." That image
shows our perverse, collective glee at somebody else's pain.
Plus overhearing other families' dramas forms a big part of
that memoir; what worried children often worry about is not
seen but overheard.

8 | Hucksters, the Deluded, and Big Fat Liars

I saw prophets tearing their false beards
I saw frauds joining sects of flagellants
executioners in sheep's clothing
who fled the people's wrath
playing shepherd's pipes

Zbigniew Herbert, "What I Saw"

Maybe deceit in memoir irks me so badly because some years back I endorsed one of the biggest literary frauds in recent memory. Fake Holocaust survivor Binjamin Wilkomirski's childhood recollection of Auschwitz, *Fragments*, carries praise and my name on the British edition circa 1996. But Bruno Dösseker (Wilkomirski's birth certificate name) not only spent the war comfortably in Switzerland; he wasn't even Jewish. He began faxing his therapist "memories"—sometimes ten or twelve pages at a time as they came to him, but the therapist knew his client couldn't really discern between reality and fantasy. "If he'd called the piece *Fragments from a Therapy* he would've been fine," the shrink said in Philip Gourevitch's *New Yorker* exposé "The Memory Thief."

Now the book's falsehoods seem so glaring. Wilkomirski would've had to be Superman or made of rubber to endure what he alleges—one of the most unrelentingly brutal journeys ever set in ink. He claimed that at age three he hung by his teeth from a guard's bicep. No such jaw strength exists outside the circus, plus the guard would have to be holding his arm upside down, bicep to the ground, while supporting the iron-jawed toddler. Riding on a conveyor belt headed for the ovens under naked corpses, he feels two disembodied hands appear, rescuing him from the incinerator in the last second. All of this he bounces up from, charging at the next Nazi he sees like a rabid Chihuahua.

Some part of me I stifled knew it was false, but I still got behind the book. Why? Was I just cowed by its resounding international endorsement? More driving, I think now, was the guilt I'd suffer if it *were* true, and I denied a camp survivor his witnessing. I just didn't let myself trust my instincts.

I was in good company. Wilkomirski would go on to win the Prix de Mémoire de la Shoah in Paris and a National Jewish Book Award in NYC, where he beat out Elie Wiesel and Alfred Kazin. Also blurbing the book alongside me was biographer and investigative journalist Gitta Sereny, who attended the Nuremberg trials and wrote perhaps the definitive bio of Albert Speer.

Today, Wilkomirski cleaves unswerving to his story, unbudged by physical evidence. If the guy was attempting to defraud us, Gourevitch claimed, he did the worst job in history, for clues abounded. Wilkomirski sounds more deranged than like a conscious fake.

In one of my most depressing exercises in public naïveté,

I've handed out to classes two unidentified chapters from two Holocaust memoirs—one Primo Levi's agonizingly true *Survival at Auschwitz*, one Wilkomirski's. The proven fabricator gets the vast majority of votes for veracity every time.

Here are the reasons my very smart (some Ivy-educated) grad students give for taking all this in as true.

1. He's not trying to make himself seem like a hero. (I'd disagree: he's making himself seem like a victim, which translates into survivor, which translates into hero.)
2. Why would he lie about this? (He seems to believe his lies, according to his shrink and Gourevitch, who interviewed him.)
3. The writing has an immediacy; its first-person present tense makes it seem as if he's reliving it, more than Levi's more formally written piece with its emotional circumspection.
4. Lack of exposition or rhetoric shows lack of thoughtfulness and, therefore, a lack of artificiality or deceit.
5. The writing is more conversational than Levy's—informality equals truth to many students.
6. It's fragmentary, like traumatic memory or a movie flashback.
7. He puts in dialogue. Whereas Levi, the real survivor, is more sparing with dialogue, Wilkomirski has long conversations.
8. Levi uses too many proper names—how could he recall them all? (I assume he's smart, or maybe he looked some up.)
9. Levi sounds too upper-crust or smart, which makes students see him as posed; they find the informality

of Wilkomirski's writing winning. (They also have this complaint with lefty Orwell—he sounds too highbrow!)

10. What if it's true, and we don't believe him?

In 2008, of eighteen students, only three found Levi the more plausible; in 2012, of twenty-one students, three again found Levi more plausible. Which means to me that reasonable judgment is still losing ground.

In cheating the public, hucksters cheat themselves out of their real stories. James Frey must've fought to get sober before *A Million Little Pieces*; just not in the ways he alleged. No doubt he suffered like hell, but he somehow deluded himself that his real misery wasn't bad enough—or maybe his real character wasn't macho enough, or nice enough to warrant scrutiny. But any addict's overhaul is a nightmare. Surely his true story would've been worth a read.

Truth is less set in stone now, more mutable. We know better than ever that people lie like crazy. They probably lied a lot before, too, but now cameras and a watchdog media seem way more adroit at catching out their lies. With the web, we've got more people trying to track down the adulterer or photograph the drunk celebrity who's fallen off the wagon.

We also often believe all manner of horse dookey based on prevailing winds—family denial systems stay impregnable based on that tendency. Or we're swept up in a tale we want to believe. Millions of perfectly bright readers get drawn in and duped by bullshit stories. I fell for Lillian Hellman's self-aggrandizing tales in *Pentimento*, until Mary McCarthy—

known as a rigorous truth seeker—told Dick Cavett's television audience, "Every word out of her mouth is a lie, including *and* and *the*." Nothing protects us against practiced liars and hucksters; nothing ever will.

What rankles me lately, though, is a sweeping tendency to deny even the possibility of truth. During a campus sexual harassment investigation, my department chair said, "There's her version and his version—there is no truth." Which infuriated me: someone either assaulted the woman in question, or not. It was binary.

Sure, there are major mistakes of interpretation. Two cops beating a black man claim he was reaching for a weapon in his pants. A video shows the victim groping, but it's for an asthma inhaler.

In an off-kilter paradox, our strange cynicism about truth as a possibility has permitted us to accept all manner of bullshit on the page. Or maybe our appetite for the fantastic—fed by *Ironman* and *Gravity* and a phalanx of vampire- and zombie-based blockbusters—has eroded all public standards of plausibility, even among perfectly smart people. (Okay, there are some dumb bunnies. Walking out of *The Last Temptation of Christ*, a friend overheard someone say, "I didn't know Jesus was so short.") Our desire for spectacle has led many story-concocting "memoirists" into jacking up their tales, believing that the story with the most gunshots will win the biggest audience.

But it's the busted liars who talk most volubly about the fuzzy line between nonfiction and fiction. Their anything-goes message has come to dominate the airwaves around memoir.

Reading that scammer James Frey got on a plane with a bullet hole through his cheek, I deduced that—even pre-9/11— airport security frowned on boarding the gunshot-wounded.

And when he alleged that his rehab made him suffer a root canal without a non-consciousness-altering numbing agent, sober people the world over knew the torture session was fake. The bullet hole and unnumbed tooth were absolute tip-offs. Surely other readers, had they paused even for a second to consider the unlikelihood of those reports, would have dubbed the guy a bullshitter.

What I'm guessing: many just shrugged past it, because we've all chosen to accept that the line between fiction and nonfiction is too subtle for us to discern. That's what Frey argued on TV, vigorously. He had no reluctance to speak for all memoirists, claiming self-righteously to both Oprah and Larry King that his form of shameless "embellishment" was customary for all memoir, since the genre's so "new" (are you listening St. Augustine?). His self-righteous defense and total lack of apology might have tipped us off that we were dealing with a practiced dissembler.

Of course, there was no way for any of us to deduce what he flat-out lied about. He transformed his frat boy's DUI with its $733 bail and few hours sipping coffee in an Ohio police station into a month-long jail sentence—the result of this roostering desperado's fistfight with cops and all manner of trumped-up charges. His college-educated girlfriend became a crack whore since puberty. And he claimed "I stand by my book" partly because the lies occupied only eighteen pages, or 5 percent of it—"within the realm of what's appropriate in memoir."

To follow his reasoning, an event manufactured from whole cloth is the moral equivalent of another memoirist blurring identity to disguise someone or misremembering a date.

This isn't quite true. The line between *memory* and *fact* is blurry, between *interpretation* and *fact*. There are inadvertent mistakes of those kinds out the wazoo. But Frey didn't "misremember" and actually believe he had a bullet wound. He didn't really believe he was incarcerated for months, when he never served a day. He set out to fool people.

So did Greg Mortenson, the skunk-posing-as-saint builder of Afghan schools in *Three Cups of Tea*. He didn't hallucinate that he'd been kidnapped by Taliban when, in fact, he'd been hosted in some kind people's homes. He cooked up events to mold his public image into that of the noble, forgiving survivor of brutal treatment. Jon Krakauer's *Three Cups of Deceit* details how Mortenson went on to drain massive sums from his charity for personal use, renting private jets for book-selling junkets and buying his own books at retail to stay on best-seller lists. He was forced by the Montana attorney general to repay $1,000,000 to settle the allegations. Yet as recently as January 2014, I saw Mortenson use the same smarmy, indeterminate nonconfession that once came out of James Frey's mouth: "I made some mistakes."

I'm not trying to make lie-sniffing bloodhounds out of memoir fans, nor to silence would-be memoirists who give up the art, fearing their minds aren't as steadfast as computer files and video footage. I don't yearn for some golden age of objective truth when the fact police patrolled dialogue in memoir, demanding it be excised unless the writer had recorded backup. But the popular, scoffing presumption that memory's solely concocted by self-serving fantasy and everyone's trying to scudge has perhaps helped to bog down our collective moral machinery.

Our reigning, collective suspicion has extended the practiced liars' motives to everyone, including the well-intentioned truth seeker. In so doing, we've let a small cadre of schemers take over. Disgraced con men have helped to author the dominant notion that a thinking person can't possibly discern between a probable truth and a hyperembellished swindle. Based on their antics, we've begun to abandon all judgment, thinking instead, Oh, who knows, anything's possible, everybody lies anyway.

My heroes in the fields of memoir and journalism don't find the line so indeterminate. Hilary Mantel still shoots for undiluted reality: "I have an investment in accuracy. I would never say, 'It doesn't matter, it's history now.' " And David Carr outlined this once-simple standard in "Journalist Dancing on the Edge of Truth," where he indicts shamed *New Yorker* writer Jonah Lehrer for making up quotes from Bob Dylan: "Every reporter who came up in legacy media can tell you about a come-to-Jesus moment when an editor put them up against a wall and tattooed a message deep into their skull: show respect for the fundamentals of the craft, or you would not soon be part of it. I once lost a job I dearly wanted because I had misspelled the name of the publisher of the publication I was about to go to work for. Not very smart, but I learned a brutal lesson that stayed with me." (*New York Times*, August 19, 2012)

However often the airwaves wind up clotted with false memories and misidentified criminal culprits and folks dithering about what they recall, I still think a screw has come loose in our culture around notions of truth, a word you almost can't set down without quotes around it anymore. Sometimes it strikes me that even when we *know* something's true, it's almost rude to say so, as if claiming a truth at all—what? threatens someone else's experience? Most of all, no one wants to sound like some self-satisfied proselytizer everybody can pounce on and debunk.

The American religion—so far as there is one anymore—
seems to be doubt. Whoever believes the least wins, because
he'll never be found wrong.

It is odd that I've never seen a televised minute about the
simple rules of veracity the nonfiction writers I know seem
to cleave to, murdering themselves in revision after revision
trying to meet it.

This overlooks the reality—am I the only person left alive
to believe this?—that most memoirists know the past can be a
swamp. Nonetheless, most are trying to find footing on more
solid ground. Some memories—often the best and worst—
burn inside us for lifetimes, florid, unforgettable, demanding
to be set down.

9 | Interiority and Inner Enemy—Private Agonies Read Deeper Than External Whammies

> *It is a misfortune, in some senses: I feed too much on*
> *the inward sources; I live too much with the dead.*
> *My mind is something like the ghost of an ancient,*
> *wandering about the world and trying mentally*
> *to construct it as it used to be, in spite of ruin and*
> *confusing changes. But I find it necessary to use the*
> *utmost caution about my eyesight.*
>
> George Eliot, *Middlemarch*

Carnality may determine whether a memoir's any good, but interiority—that kingdom the camera never captures—makes a book rereadable. By rereadable, translate: great. Your connection to most authors usually rests (Nabokov and a few others aside) in how you may identify with them. Mainly, the better memoirist organizes a life story around that aforementioned inner enemy—a psychic struggle against herself that works like a thread or plot engine.

Interiority moves us through the magic realms of time and truth, hope and fantasy, memory, feelings, ideas, worries.

Emotions you can't show carnally are told. Whenever a writer gets reflective about how she feels or complains or celebrates or plots or judges, she moves inside herself to where things matter and mean.

Early on in a childhood tale, an author may render consciousness awakening—that enduring, often-trivial first memory, through which a narrator blinks into being. Nabokov made such a moment so singular, its machinery almost speaks to or sparks my own such arrival, as if he described something I, too, had felt but never been able to articulate: "I see the awakening of consciousness as a series of spaced flashes, with the intervals between them gradually diminishing until bright blocks of perception are formed, affording memory a slippery hold." As you watch the narrator feel around the edges of consciousness for its "slippery hold"—probing for what really went down—you enter a singular set of psychic perceptions. But craving that "hold" or permanence in what's past is Nabokov's inner enemy.

Even a writer with gargantuan external enemies must face off with himself over a book's course. Otherwise, why write in first person at all?

The split self or inner conflict must manifest on the first pages and form the book's thrust or through line—some journey toward the self's overhaul by book's end. However random or episodic a book seems, a blazing psychic struggle holds it together, either thematically or in the way a plot would keep a novel rolling forward. Often the inner enemy dovetails with the writer's own emotional investment in the work at hand. Why is she driven to tell the tale? Usually it's to go back and recover some lost aspect of the past so it can be integrated into current identity.

Frank Conroy's inner enemy is his inability to maintain balance and control in the chaotic world of his feckless family without either disassociation or rebelling in self-destructive ways. *Stop-Time* shows the power of spacing out to protect a kid in pain. That inner blankness or emptiness provides the place where Conroy—a professional jazz pianist when I knew him—could shape "music" or form out of his environment's painful disorder. He enacts how a deprived kid *survives*, not just suffers, and it's through disassociation—a consciousness leaving time and place.

> For an hour or more I lay motionless in a self-induced trance, my eyes open but seldom moving. . . . In this state my ears seemed rather far away. I was burrowed somewhere deep in my skull.

And the undercurrent of the book is the aimless boredom of childhood. Since kids lack power and agency over much, they must embrace empty time. Conroy does it with bitterness.

> My philosophy, at age eleven, was skepticism. Like most children I was antisentimental and quick to hear false notes. I waited, more than anything else, waited for something momentous to happen. Keeping a firm grip on reality was of immense importance. My vision had to be clear so that when "it" happened I would know. . . . (A spectacularly unsuccessful philosophy since nothing ever happened.)

As his reckless parents and lackluster teachers failed to protect him, he gradually "slipped into the state of being in trouble." The book opens with him as an adult driving drunk at a hundred miles per hour from London to his home in the suburbs. His outlaw streak, which we grow to love him for, also endangers him.

For Harry Crews, his fatherless state somehow cuts him off from forging a solid self. He started the book "because I've never been certain of who *I* am." He's a man stripped of identity, which he can only reclaim by reabsorbing his lost home place, partly through memories of the father who grew there and then died before Crews could be born. The book's stated emotional quest is to gather and utter old stories to fill in blanks in the writer with his old man's past and peoples. Otherwise, Crews might have to move through life as an undefined shapeshifter, a kind of poppet for other people's influences. He describes himself as a guy who goes from mask to mask, "slipping into and out of identities as easily as people slip in and out of their clothes." Even the voice we find so distinctive, he claims, is actually malleable as putty: as a reporter, listening to recorded interviews with film stars or truckers after the fact, his "own voice will invariably become indistinguishable from the voice of the person with whom I'm talking by the third or fourth tape. Some natural mimic in me picks up whatever verbal tics or mannerisms it gets close to."

In his macho-named book *Blood and Grits*, he confesses the shame of trying to be a literary man when he comes from illiterate sharecroppers: "Everything I had written had been out of a fear and loathing for what I was and who I was. It was all out of an effort to pretend otherwise."

This seems the place to mention that we later find out that

Crews's mother remarried while Crews was still a baby, and so till age six, the man he called "daddy" was a violent drunk uncle who terrorized the family. Before Crews was even conceived, the father he mourns lost one testicle to the clap, while working on a dredging crew in the Florida swamps. He caught it from "a flat-faced Seminole girl whose name he never knew and who grunted like a sow and smelled like something shot in the woods."

This unflattering portrait of the unflattering act helps describe the hard place we're in—a universe full of loud pigs and shot things you have to take whiffs of while walking around. It's a world told in muscular language and jam-packed with action of the grittiest sort.

But that lost world is also one where people hang tough together, and Crews sounds—above all else—so lonely and disconnected. That sense of unassailable community would seem to him like food to a starving man. Crews never seems to have had a pal like his daddy's on the dredging crew, a guy who took the old man to have one testicle lopped off. Before that, the friend engages the old man in a grim banter that binds them.

> The rhythmic stroke of the dredge's engine came counterpoint to my daddy's shaky voice as he told Cecil what was wrong.
> When Cecil finally did speak, he said, "I hope it was good boy. I sho do."
> "What was good?"
> "That Indian. You got the clap."
> But daddy had already known. He had thought of little else since it had become almost impossible for him to give water because of the fire that started in his stomach and felt like it burned through raw flesh

> every time he had to water off. He had thought of the
> chickee where he had lain under the palm roof being
> eaten alive by mosquitoes.

Because such stories are Crews's patrimony, the sole bonds
that tether him to the planet, the carnal reality of the place and
his daddy's suffering body have an immediacy we have to buy
into.

For the sake of his own manhood, we sense, Papa Crews
embodies the butch, hypertrophied male, and all of Crews's
tough acts—from joining the marines and brawling and
working as a carny to getting massive skull tattoos—seem
to grow from the author's longing to live up to the mythic,
über-mensch patriarch only met in photos and stories. "His is
the gun that is always drawn; his is the head that is turned
back under the whiskey bottle." That *always* is a kind of plain-
tive cry. Forgive me for getting all Freudian here, but for the
father with one testicle to have a gun that is always drawn
does sound like a son's own desperate wish for a macho old
man.

One mark of capital-M Modernism is writers commenting self-
reflexively on the fact that they're writing, as when a theater
character breaks the fourth wall and directly addresses the audience. In a conflict such as Crews's, the process of telling a
story in a way solves the psyche's core problem—in this, there's
a poetic marriage of form and content. The medium is the message. Again, we hear Mantel in *Giving Up the Ghost* wrestling
with her ability to incorporate her experience of the supernatural in a time when she'd be adjudged mad for the belief:

So now I come to write a memoir. I tell myself, just say how you came to sell a house with a ghost in it. But this story can only be told once, and I need to get it right. Why does the act of writing generate so much anxiety? Margaret Atwood says, "The written word is so much like evidence—like something that can be used against you." I used to think that autobiography was a form of weakness, and perhaps I still do. But I also think that, if you're weak, it's childish to pretend to be strong.

Unless you confess your own emotional stakes in a project, why should a reader have any? A writer sets personal reasons for the text at hand, and her struggling psyche fuels the tale. Here's me in my first book, trying to explain how what I didn't know about my past haunted me:

> When the truth would be unbearable, the mind often just blanks it out. But the ghost of the event may stay in your head. Then, like a smudge of a bad word wiped off on a school blackboard, this ghost can call undue attention to itself by its very vagueness. . . . The night's major consequences for me were internal. The fact that my house was Not Right metastasized into the notion that I myself was Not Right, or that my survival in the world depended on my constant vigilance against various forms of Not Rightness.

In *Night*, concentration camp survivor Elie Wiesel perhaps suffers as much from his own guilt about how he treated his dying father as he does from the depredations the Nazis inflict. While the sick old man in his death throes calls the author's name, the young man stays away, begrudging his father those agonized cries, which eventually draw the blows of the SS: "I shall never forgive myself. His last word had been my name. A summons. I had not responded." Yes, the camp and its tortures overwhelm Wiesel, but this internal conflict deepens the story. So it's odd to me that in later editions of the book, Wiesel cut the passage, claiming it was "Too personal, too private, perhaps . . ."

The need to rout out my own inner demons is why I always start off fumbling through my own recollections. Only later, after several drafts do I engage in "research" by visiting old haunts and passing my manuscript around. The memories I've gnawed on and rehearsed are the ones most key to what's eating me up, and only those can help me to find a book's shape.

Reading George Orwell's masterful essay "Shooting an Elephant"—for my purposes a mini memoir—you see two halves of a man colliding. He doesn't try to justify his own actions in putting down a pricey animal in Burma as a British police officer during the Raj. He's not yet the political lefty who'll fight in the Spanish Civil War and pen *1984*, but serving overseas, he's started to sour on imperialism, and to empathize for the people he's paid to repress.

On the other hand, the populace baits and torments him—they're an obvious external enemy: "In Moulmein, in lower Burma, I was hated by large numbers of people—the only time in my life I have been important enough for this to happen to me."

But the inner struggle that shapes the piece is how that hatred begins to warp his insides. Orwell's own malice eats him up, so that he writes of the mocking young monks who languish on the streets and tea bars to tease him, "[I] thought that the greatest joy in the world would be to drive a bayonet into a Buddhist priest's guts."

If you haven't read the piece, it follows a simple thread. An elephant in rut goes mad and kills a coolie. But by the time the crowd has jeered and cajoled Orwell into rushing to the scene, the calm, sleepy-looking critter is pulling up grass to eat. As he beats the dusty roots on his knees to get the dirt off, Orwell observes he has a "preoccupied grandmotherly air." Still, the crowd bullies Orwell into shooting the elephant with a rifle so small he has to fire over and over while the thing gasps and coughs gouts of blood. It's one of the most personally indicting scenes in memoir I've ever come across.

> When I pulled the trigger I did not hear the bang
> or feel the kick—one never does when the shot goes
> home—but I heard the devilish roar of glee that
> went up from the crowd. . . . [A] mysterious, terrible
> change had come over the elephant. He neither
> stirred nor fell, but every line of his body had altered.
> He looked suddenly stricken, shrunken, immensely
> old. . . . [He] sagged flabbily to his knees. His mouth
> slobbered.

What was happening to Orwell at that time—the schism inside between disgust at his role in the Raj and his fury at the Burmese who hated him for his role—forges the story. As he says near the end, "You wear a mask, and your face grows to fit it." He offers himself no mercy with the ironic end statement that he was glad the animal had killed a coolie for "it put me legally in the right," adding, "I had done it solely to avoid looking the fool."

Try to think of Orwell writing the story solely as someone sympathetic to the Burmese people, and there'd be no emotional power to what he was telling. He'd come off as someone selfishly defending his own actions. Once the reader identifies a vain or self-serving streak the writer can't admit to with candor, a level of distrust interferes with that reader's experience. In almost every literary memoir I know, it's the internal struggle providing the engine for the tale. Orwell's powers of description wring emotion from a reader for all players—the animal, the people, and the callow young police officer lost in fear and pride. Yes, the elephant embodies that old-school battle with nature that powered so many great novels, but it also mirrors Orwell's inner war.

10 | On Finding the Nature of Your Talent

Above all, don't lie to yourself. The man who lies to himself and listens to his own lie comes to a point where he cannot distinguish the truth within him or around him, and so loses respect for himself. And having no respect, he ceases to love.

Fyodor Dostoevsky

I often find students in early pages showing themselves exactly opposite from how they actually are. The talented young poet who didn't want to bring her passionately felt love poems because they felt too "girlie" was an engagingly vulnerable and girlie individual. The superbrainiac tried posing as a working-class hero. One of the sweetest kids I ever knew wrote like a sociopathic hardass. Trying to help students diagnose their own blind spots, I often ask the following questions:

1. What do people usually like and dislike about you? You should reflect both aspects in your pages.
2. How do you want to be perceived, and in what ways have you ever been false or posed as other than who

you are? (Lovers/family yelling at you when they're mad have answered this one for you, btw.)

3. Is there any verbal signpost you can look for that suggests you're posturing? One kid I know started bringing in references to metal bands to show how cool he was. I might start yakking about philosophy.

Any reader could answer these questions on my behalf, I think:

1. My friends usually like me because I'm tenderhearted, blunt, salty, and curious. I'm super loyal, and I laugh loud.

2. People don't like me because I'm emotionally intense and often cross boundaries—sometimes inadvertently, other times just being puckish. My disposition tends toward dark. Small talk at parties bores me senseless, and at weddings I prefer to dance rather than chitchat. I'm a little bit of a misanthrope. I cancel lunch dates because I'm working.

3. I'd love the cool voice of an emotionally reticent intellectual. My role in my family was to feel, so I was initially scared to feel on the page. Doing so felt too bald and lunkheaded. But when I get away from felt moments or stories, I'm giving up what I'm better at.

4. When I start digressing into highfalutin diction about intellectual subjects I know nothing about.

In short: How are you trying to appear? The author of a lasting memoir manages to power past the initial defenses, digging past the false self to where the truer one waits to tell the more complicated story.

11 | The Visionary Maxine Hong Kingston

We know the truth not only by reason but also by heart.

Blaise Pascal, *Pensées*

Maxine Hong Kingston's oddly ethereal vision helped forge the genre of memoir as we know it, and her *Woman Warrior*, published in 1975, stands today on the shelves of most college bookstores and libraries. After three decades of teaching her, I still marvel at how she enthralls my students. The two prongs of her massive talent mirror the two sides of the story's conflict—her truth-hungry, feminist, Americanized self does battle with her mother's repressive notions of Chinese ladylikeness and humility.

From the book's first breath, the writer betrays a confidence from her mother, a secret born of ancient cultural values that define what being a woman should embody—mostly eating a big shit sandwich with a servile smile on your face. "Better to raise geese than girls" is one piece of wisdom, and infanticide for girl babies is accepted practice. So the writer sets her own blabby, American-educated mouth against her mother's traditional ideas of feminine modesty, clan loyalty, and demure comportment—her struggle throughout the book. The book opens with both the mother's admonishing voice and—in the very act of reporting that voice—the daughter's broken covenant. In this exquisite ventriloquism, the two opponents start off speaking through the same mouth:

> "You must not tell anyone," my mother said, "what I am about to tell you. In China your father had a sister who killed herself. She jumped into the family well. We say that your father has all brothers because it is as if she had never been born."

Before this nameless aunt drowns herself in the well, she turns up in the fields pregnant, though her husband has been gone too long to have fathered the baby. In a savage, hallucinatory attack, the villagers ransack the family home, stealing their rice and slaughtering their livestock to punish the family for the aunt's shame. That night the aunt bears her bastard in a pigsty, and in the morning the family finds her and the baby "plugging up the family well."

Hong Kingston's mother relays the aunt's story to warn the young author—who's just gotten her period and thus reached the age to bring shame—away from sex, away from appetite, away from opening her mouth at all. To be forgotten is to be condemned to an eternal hell without family. Forgotten ancestors are "hungry ghosts," unfed because they're unremembered.

Part of Hong Kingston's originality springs from her poetic marriage of form and content: the conflict raging between the two cultures within the young speaker shapes the book's flip-flops between realism and fantasy. Transgressing against the Chinese tradition of female silence, she spills family secrets and displays a hunger for truth that makes her almost as dangerous as her shamed aunt. She appropriates as a birthright her mother's method of fable or "talk story" to fantasize about who that lost aunt might have been. Hong Kingston makes it clear she's not doling out facts, just speculating on the dramatic possibilities. At first she imagines the drowned aunt as a rape victim, assaulted in the field, too ashamed to complain. Or maybe she was raped by a family member. Hong Kingston also fashions her as an outlaw: a vain and lovesick tart, "a wild woman" who "kept rollicking company."

Saving the aunt from oblivion, Hong Kingston saves herself from being constricted by the old ways like a foot bound in silk.

> I alone devote pages of paper to her, though not origamied into houses and clothes. I do not think she always means me well. I am telling on her, and she was a spite suicide, drowning herself in the drinking water. The Chinese are always very frightened of the drowned one, whose weeping ghost, wet hair hanging down and skin bloated, waits silently by the water to pull down a substitute.

Later, in adolescence, Hong Kingston begins to try to turn herself "American feminine": proud, standing tall with toes out, not the humble and silent, hunched-over and pigeon-toed "Chinese feminine."

> What is Chinese and what is movies. The danger in China was the ancestors. The danger in America are

the children. They inherit the ghosts' sins and are
bloated and hungry.

She grows into a recklessly defiant daughter and a school
bully, trying to pinch and torment a shy student into speech.

Hong Kingston's lurid fantasy sequences echo her mother's supernatural tales. While reviews at the time likened passages of
The Woman Warrior to the then-new Latin American magical
realism of, say, Gabriel García Márquez, Hong Kingston's work
is far more supernatural than realistic. Facing danger, her
mother could metamorphose into a dragon: "[She] fanned out
her dragon claws and riffled her red sequin scales." She flew
over cloudscapes.

Contrast such transformations with García Márquez's
grounded-in-physical-reality scenarios from *One Hundred Years
of Solitude*, which opens with the explainable "magic" of scientific invention—ice in the tropics, say, or a magnet so powerful
it draws nails from houses as it's dragged down the street. In
García Márquez, a dead man's dentures sprout yellow flowers
in his toothglass, and butterflies appear in the presence of a
great beauty. "Surreal?" García Márquez once quipped. "That's
how life is in South America." He makes the magical credible,
then, step by step, leads the reader into the ghostly.

Hong Kingston's book feels dreamier, bolder in how it challenges a reader's credulity. She starts off with physically possible events, then eventually you must leap into an enchanted
village structure where "spirits shimmered among the live
creatures." But given how the writer wrestles throughout
her California childhood with the mysterious constraints of

the ancient world, the ghostly comes off as the truest way to render her internal dramas. She doesn't know what to believe and what's myth. The family actually refers to their American neighbors as "ghosts"; it's family wisdom that, as an emigrant child, she's being devoured by this ghost culture, so her parents hide things from her.

> Sometimes I hated the ghosts for not letting us talk;
> sometimes I hated the secrecy of the Chinese. "Don't
> tell," said my parents, though we couldn't tell if we
> wanted to because we didn't know. They would not
> tell us children because we had been born among
> ghosts, were taught by ghosts, and were ourselves
> ghost-like.

Mysterious rituals are enacted and never talked about. At dinner, "Mother would pour Seagram's 7 into the cups and, after a while, pour it back into the bottle. Never explaining."

Ironically, the adoption of her mother's fantasy technique also serves this memoirist as an unlikely form of discretion. Because of it, the family secrets are kept, in a way; the book is a demimonde where reality and myth blur.

That uncertain whimsy in another writer's book would rankle or bore, coming off as digressive or decorative. Attempting to use Hong Kingston's method myself, I could too easily hear a reader saying, *Get back to the* real *story*, as I tried to bamboozle her with pages of witchy spirits and conjecture. But Hong Kingston dissects its cultural source and context. As she explains how the fantastic became real in her household, we accept the mystical instant as wholly natural, as in this stranger-than-fiction trip to the drive-in:

> There was the woman next door who was chatty
> one moment—inviting us children to our first "sky
> movie"—and shut up the rest. Then we would see
> silver heat rise from her body; it solidified before our
> eyes. . . . Her husband threw the loudspeaker out the
> window and drove home fast.

The girl matter-of-factly watches this angry spirit rise from a woman's body. Few other writers could get away with this—it'd feel like technique. In Hong Kingston's hands, it comes off as "true," because the world she's constructed operates that way.

She takes neighborhood rumor about a corpse-strewn landscape and locates it in an actual physical place. Once you accept this fantastic premise, believing in the local witch isn't far off.

> People had been known to have followed hobo paths
> [into a slough] and parted the stalks to find dead
> bodies—hoboes, Chinese suicides, children. . . . Kids
> said [this madwoman] was a witch capable of witch
> deeds, unspeakable boilings and tearings apart and
> transformations if she caught us. "She'll touch you on
> the shoulder, and you'll not be you anymore. You'd be
> a piece of glass winking and blinking to people on the
> sidewalk." She came riding to the slough with a broom
> between her legs, and she had powdered one cheek
> red and one white. Her hair stood up and out to the
> side in dry masses, black even though she was old. She
> wore a pointed hat and layers of capes, shawls, sweaters
> buttoned at the throat like capes, the sleeves flying
> behind like sausage skins.

She starts the awful scene of realistically dead bodies among the cattails. Then she moves to apocrypha—kids saying she could transform you. Then she launches into the fabulist.

Yet such fables tell truths that would otherwise go unspoken. In a culture that may strike an American reader as shadowed by concealment, the mythic serves as a form of sidewinding candor. Once Hong Kingston shows you how to read her, you don't care whether you're in mythville or on reality. com because some part of you has yielded to her methods. Over the course of the book, you master swimming fluidly between both realms.

Some scenes are so thematically perfect and physically bizarre, the reader doubts them though they're possible. Before Hong Kingston started speaking in her American school, she claims, she took an IQ test and secured "a zero IQ." As part of a cure for her daughter's silence, which meant failure in her American school, Hong Kingston's mother went into the young writer's mouth with scissors, cutting the small membrane under her tongue called the frenum, thus "freeing her tongue" for speech. The particularity of the event argues for actuality, but its perfect match with the book's themes of feminine silence argues for myth.

While I couldn't directly copy Hong Kingston's method in my own first book, studying her gave me the courage to use the Texas tall tales I'd overheard from my daddy and his gambling buddies. After a cold ride in a boxcar, a man finds a frozen, slightly fuzzy object rolling from his pant leg. Thawed in a frying pan, it makes a fart noise. But such a joke from me comes off as just that: a joke. No one would call it a witnessed event. Hong Kingston's mystical swordswomen somehow become living creatures.

The truth of a writer's self—Hong Kingston's penchant for fabulism, say—has a way of bobbing up on the pages like a badly weighted corpse. You may as well bring the reader to the swampy grave from the git-go.

Back in the 1970s, Hong Kingston transgressed against a culture of silence to overlay Chinese myth and ancient texts onto a modern landscape. It was a feminist act, revealing secrets in order to free herself and the women of her clan from the silence and obscurity to which a misogyny thousands of years old would have relegated them. While the book hit best-seller lists and got raves, its writer was often trounced in reviews by male Asian scriveners whose own lesser works sank into deserved obscurity. Frank Chin scolded her and my friend Amy Tan (among others) for restating white stereotypes in their work. Tan recently noted vis-à-vis Chin's attacks that "Being marginalized by the reading public was adjudged authentic by him, whereas being read by the mainstream invariably meant you'd sold out."

While I can't speak with authority to the issues of inequality Chin seems (rightly) fired up about, I must defend Hong Kingston's right to represent her own Chinese girlhood any way she damn pleases, without checking with the male thought police first. Amy Tan put it this way: "Sure, you can establish tidy moral or political standards for how race is represented on the page: it's called propaganda." Propaganda seeks to destroy art in order to sanitize culture. Hong Kingston's *Woman Warrior* has outlived the past's more sexist environment to win the ardor of generations. It's a timeless monument to memoir's possibilities.

12 | Dealing with Beloveds (On and Off the Page)

Families exist to witness each other's disappointments.

Laura Sillerman

Methods for dealing with family and friends differ as radically as writers do. On one end sit memoirists—mostly women—who interview and almost collaborate. Carolyn See rewrote her *Dreaming* in response to family comment. On the other sit those with enough moxie not to give a rat's ass—all men, in my experience. Frank Conroy claimed he did *Stop-Time* without much interest in his own clan's response at all. "If they'd have disapproved, I wouldn't have changed a word." My friend Jerry Stahl, whose *Permanent Midnight* challenged family history by renaming his father's death a suicide, once said, "If you had to live it, you get to write it."

The gender divide makes sense. Men can become men by rebelling against their folks—the angry young rock-and-roller stealing the car or standing up to the patriarch is an archetype—Oedipus slaying his father to marry his mother. But for a woman to kick her mother's ass is unseemly. When I half chastised Lucy Grealy for—in her *Autobiography of a Face*—not explaining why her family seemingly abandoned her in the UK during the agonizing cancer treatments she underwent as a teen, she said, "Women are repositories of clan lore, and our femininity is gauged by the security of family relationships. To drag out the dirty laundry almost masculinizes a woman." Of course we gossip and worry stories with each other in ways that would horrify many of our male kinfolk. But publishing such gossip, Lucy suggested, was something much worse.

Geoffrey Wolff bemoaned the effects of *Duke* on his prim mother, who'd been called a nasty name by a scumbag reviewer. "After that," he'd told me, "it was clear she wished the book had never existed." He particularly warned me off TV talk shows where complex family issues get warped into sound bites:

> You take the people you love most in the world and make them characters in a narrative. Then you lose control of that narrative. . . . Dick Cavett found my life droll.

Then Toby's book came out to wild acclaim. I'd twice met their mother—immaculately coiffed and tiny. I sat behind them all in the movie version of *This Boy's Life*. She's played by a chirpy Ellen Barkin, Toby by Leo DiCaprio; De Niro does the awful stepdad. Toby had to urge the director to edit out a supersexual part. "How could I have witnessed such a thing!" The *New York Times Magazine* quoted Geoffrey as saying:

> Here's this woman—she's been written about once. The train's rolled over her going north. She picks

herself up and dusts herself off, and here comes the
train about to back over her.

Mother Wolff's quip: "If I'd known both my boys were
going to be writers, I might have lived a little differently."

Now comes the juncture where I either detail my own travails
with others or end the chapter. The trusty literary advisers I
call my Kitchen Cabinet have warned me off spending time
here on my own processes. Maybe any writer who yaps about
her work outside brief interviews comes off as a car salesman.
Or worse, as if she's touting herself as the doyenne. Believe me,
I'm not—no one can be. It's all too personal. Yet I don't know
anyone else's adventures with family as intimately as my own,
and not to include them seems coy at best, deceitful at worst.
So here goes.

In general terms, there are three parts to my handling of
others. I notify them way in advance, to give them a chance
to shoot it down (nobody has yet). I keep pages private till the
book's done, and at the end, I send work out to folks I wrote
about long before type's set. As a side note, it's not my nature to
write at any length about people I don't like. Save portraits of a
grandmother who pissed me off and two pedophiles, it's mostly
love that drives me to the page.

My son was in junior high when my second memoir came
out, and he took a stance he held for more than a decade: "I'm
not ready to read your books." This strikes me as wise. It's one
thing to know your mother was sexually assaulted, quite another to read the graphic scene. He prefers me as a dispenser of
waffles, not a literary figure. But there's nothing in my stories

he doesn't know in rough outline—we're close, and I'd never want him to hear family traumas from pals. With my last book, *Lit*, I had him vet the first chapter, because he appeared there in his then-current, college-age permutation. He changed nary a word. I'd have preferred that his father scrutinize that manuscript for accuracy, but he preferred the blurring of a pseudonym. (I did send those chapters to our former marriage counselor, just to see if she felt it fair.)

Glib as I once was in suggesting Lucy Grealy piss off her own family, I was much like her before I set out to write about my less-than-perfect clan. As a single mom far from home, I dreaded pissing anybody off.

Before I ever started *Liars' Club*, I kept phoning my mother and sister (my daddy had passed) to take their pulses about the project and warn them about possible public scrutiny, should I be so lucky as to draw any.

Part of me hoped they'd shoo me off. Much as I worshiped the form of memoir, the project's prospect shot me through with dread. I felt compelled to write it, yet broke a sweat when I realized how easy it would be to do it wrong. Truth was, I had a financial flamethrower on my ass: no car in Syracuse, where the snow's measurable in yards, and child-care costs that precluded my making much on summer holidays.

Maybe my mother and sister were so glib about the book because they were used to my small-press poetry efforts, with readership measurable in the dozens. I knew my New York publisher hoped for world domination.

My family's unflappability worried me more than if they'd thrown fits. "Who cares?" my sister said. "Get it off your chest," my mother said. They were both great readers, and I'd been giving memoirs as gifts for decades, so they knew I was shooting for a 3D portrait, not a burn-your-house-down tell-all.

Still, our household had been the site of some flaming jackpots. Asked once how a bullet hole landed in a kitchen tile, Mother said, succinctly, "He moved." And that wasn't the only firearm incident. My sister once quipped to Mother as the tile guy fingered a bullet hole, "Isn't that where you shot at Daddy?" and Mother came back, "No, that's where I shot at Larry. Over there's where I shot at your daddy."

(Which also tells you why memoir suited me. With characters this good, why make shit up?)

But alcohol and firearms weren't the whole story—they seldom are. There was deliverance, too, thanks in no small measure to how Mother sobered up in her sixties (which showed me the way years later). Sobriety hadn't undone our tattered past, but it had worked as triage to stop the bleeding. And unearthing Mother's long-nurtured lies had led to our greatest closeness as a clan.

It pleased me no end that my family anticipated a loving portrait. And we'd spent decades clearing the ground by talking over the book's events anyway—my therapists (plural) had urged me into those conversations. Still, my family didn't seem to be twigging to the possibilities. Maybe their spectacular denial systems had kicked in again.

So at Christmas I flew down and spent several days detailing stuff I feared would embarrass them. "Remember when you brandished a butcher knife at us and set our toys on fire and got taken capital-A away?"

"Oh, hell," Mother said, "the whole town knew about that."

Lucky is the memoirist like me, blessed with a wild-ass mother: "If I gave a shit what people thought, I'd have been baking cookies and going to the PTA." She'd raised hell and knocked over supermarket displays. Plus she was a portraitist trained in New York, so she understood how point of view and feeling shape reality. She knew my voice would ground the reader in subjective reality, not feign absolute authority.

It was my in-some-ways conformist sister who came off as way too devil-may-care—but with an edge. A local insurance agent, she cussed like a sailor and acted the badass. But she'd always colored in the lines way more than the rest of us—somebody had to, I guess. She'd been naive enough to quip, repeatedly and with cheer, "I didn't have to go to therapy because you went for me." She belonged to Rotary and the women's Masonic organization. Even in the 1970s, her jeans had military creases. During her first marriage to a guy we called the Rice Baron, she once forbade me to visit their country club in my thrift-store clothes: "I wouldn't sod my yard dressed like that."

I was left, she was hard right. I was a boho loner, she a southern business owner with a Christmas card list in the high hundreds.

But despite schisms between us well into adulthood, in childhood she'd been my hero, and so would she be in the book.

After a few days in Texas, I brought up the only news the book would carry, which didn't involve them, really—two childhood sexual assaults I'd kept to myself. The morning I unburdened myself, the news went by in the blip I'd expected. Mother said, somewhat fiercely, "Those sons of bitches."

Then, after a brief lull, Lecia grabbed her purse. "I could really go for some Mexican food." Over lunch she talked about a guy who'd tried to force himself on her and how she'd physically overthrown him.

Otherwise, that ended the discussion until the night before I left, when some business acquaintance of Lecia's I barely knew came by and wanted to talk to me about the assaults. Lecia had told him the whole story. His sole question—"Were you penetrated?"—felt coldly prurient. But I figured if I were going to write a memoir, I'd better get used to it. You can't sign up to play football then whine you've been hit.

In the two-plus years I was writing, I kept the pages to myself, but occasionally I rang Mother to check out a fact—usually a date—or to take her temperature on how she felt about certain details going public. God bless her, she never blinked.

As for how I handled interpretative differences, it may not work for everybody. If somebody's view wholly opposed mine, I mentioned it in passing, yet never felt duty-bound to represent it. For instance, my blond sister adored our fair grandmother, who loved Lecia's blond ass back. I baldly showed my own scorn for the old lady (who thought my dark hair made me look Mexican—a blight) yet allowed as how my sister tatted lace with her and more or less sucked up. I also mentioned that my grandmother was dying of cancer in her fifties, which can't do much for your disposition, and a tumor the size of a grapefruit in her brain no doubt warped her disposition. In any event, I doubt the reader accepts my hatred of her as just or fair, only that it *was* my view. Here's another such mitigating passage:

> Lecia contends I started screaming, and that my
> screaming caused Mother to wheel around. . . . (Were
> Lecia writing this memoir, I would only appear in

one of three guises: sobbing hysterically, wetting my pants in a deliberately inconvenient way, or biting somebody, usually her, with no provocation.)

In short, I tried to lay out my prejudices and gesture there might be another opinion.

Once the manuscript was done, I flew Mother up to Syracuse, where she sat reading pages on the back porch. Off and on, she cried, "I was such an asshole," which shattered me in one way, but (I have to confess it) also satisfied me in another. Ultimately, she said something that rattled me to my core: "I didn't know you felt this way."

I also met Lecia in Colorado to do what we called the Child Abuse Tour. She flipped pages while I drove around old haunts, double-checking physical details. It shocked me how she wolfed the book down. "How did you remember all this shit?" She'd phoned my editor of her own volition to rave about the pages and endorse their truth, as my mother had.

A few months before the book came out, Lecia decided she was pissed off and stopped speaking to me. Though this was a fairly common phenomenon, it still set me back. But I also figured she'd be such a hero to anybody who read the story, she'd come around once it was published.

Then a writer friend figured out a way to label the book fiction and write her out, making me an only child. No doubt my mother passed this prospect along to my sister, and not long after, the publisher's lawyers reported that my sister had phoned to champion the book's accuracy again. She ultimately sold copies from her car trunk and bragged her ass off about it.

I can also honestly say that publishing the story freed us from our old shame somehow. My beautiful, outlaw seventy-year-old mother received marriage proposals from strangers; my sister was heralded as brave in every review. People wrote how my hard-drinking daddy was now their favorite patriarch.

In my hometown, the seamier facts had been common knowledge anyway, but something about having all the bad news out in open air freed us even more. Call it aversion therapy: we seemed collectively to get over Mother's half-century-plus lies about who she was. When she arranged a book signing at our local library, over five hundred people showed—including old beaus, far-flung cousins, and my first-grade teacher. In some ways, that day, with my mother and sister holding court, meant more than any good review I ever got—truly a life highlight. It burned away some old aura of shame, I think.

Which phenomenon echoes my favorite reconciliation story from Maxine Hong Kingston. Her mother couldn't believe how well Maxine had captured a village life she'd never lived. And when her later *China Men* was translated into Chinese so her father could read it, he started writing poems again in its margins, which in Chinese books are superwide to permit commentary, part of an old Confucian tradition. If Maxine was complaining about how her people devalue daughters, her father penned a poem celebrating women's equality. These were the first poems he'd written since he'd left China to work in a laundry in this country, and Maxine's mother embroidered the characters in cloth to save them.

When I donated the books with his commentary to the library at University of California, I didn't tell my father. They gave a big party during which his marginalia were displayed in glass cases. He stood before it and said loudly, "My writing," all night so onlookers could hear.

Among all the dozens of pals and shrinks and acquaintances I've sent manuscripts to, I've never had a detractor. Which probably says more about their generosity than my accuracy, so I count myself more lucky than expert.

For the record, here are my rules for dealing with others:

1. Notify subjects way in advance, detailing parts that might make them wince. So far, no one has ever winced.

2. On pain of death, don't show pages to anybody mid-process. You want them to see your best work, polished.

3. As Hubert Selby told Jerry Stahl, "If you're writing about somebody you hate, do it with great love."

4. Related to the above: I never speak with authority about how people feel or what their motives were. I may guess at it, but I always let the reader know that's speculative. I keep the focus on my own innards.

5. If somebody's opinion of what happened wholly opposes mine, I mention it in passing without feeling obliged to represent it.

6. Don't use jargon to describe people. It's both disrespectful and bad writing. I never called my parents alcoholics; I showed myself pouring vodka down the sink. Give information in the form you received it.

7. Let your friends choose their pseudonyms.

8. Try to consider the whole time you're working how your views—especially the harsh ones—may be wrong. Correct as needed.

9. With your closest compadres and touchy material, you might sit with them (same house or town, maybe not same room) while they read pages that may be painful for them.

10. I'd cut anything that someone just flat-out denies. Then again, in my family, all the worst stuff was long confessed to before I started writing the first tome.

11. Let the reader know how subjective your point of view is. This is in some way a form of respect to your subjects, who might disagree.

13 | On Information, Facts, and Data

*The most interesting information comes from children,
for they tell all they know and then stop.*

Mark Twain

The first chapters of most memoirs are fact-packed. Facts are the meat and potatoes of writing—necessary for a meal but devoid of much innate savor. Nobody buys a memoir—except maybe those by ubiquitous celebrities—to master the cold data of someone's life. Most memoirists stand daunted by the first information-dense chapter, wondering how to cram in all that background data without the pages sounding like a shampoo bottle's list of ingredients. Informational writing tells, it doesn't show. Some writers make such great sentences that they fascinate even while dispensing facts. But mostly information is the good writer's nemesis. It yanks the reader out of scenes, away from drama and lived experience, where the reader can watch external events and interpret them on his own. Getting fed bland information is like being preached to by a schoolmarm.

That said, here's the kind of data you might need to squeeze in.

- I was fourteen and seven feet tall.
- The war's losses increased tenfold, and yet high command denied we were losing.
- The drought lasted seven years and bankrupted the family.
- His father was a banker, his mother a homemaker.

Some facts hold so much drama or psychological interest, they prompt natural curiosity and a desire to know more:

- In 1968, he shot himself with a Smith and Wesson pistol.

The most skillful writers either package facts so they hold this kind of psychological interest, or the data get palmed off in carnal scenes the reader can imagine and engage with on a physical level. In these books, you often don't notice you're being fed a string of facts. They're sprinkled into other writing like pepper—there when you need them, but otherwise invisible.

My own first drafts start with information, then I try to herd that information out of my head into a remembered or living scene. I often interview myself about how I came to an opinion. Then, rather than present an abstract judgment ("She was a thief"), I try to re-create how I came to that opinion. "She was a thief" becomes "I stared into the computer's big green eye, inside which sat the web site where my diamond bracelet was being sold, Lydia's email contact in the corner."

Some data, you may think you need to blurt out—the year, for instance. But saying, "On the news that summer, I watched the president resign before helicopters on the White House lawn" says "Nixon administration" to the reader in a slightly more fetching way. One cheap way writers try to strap on character is with T-shirt slogans and brand-name clothing. I encourage my students to work a little harder than this. Try to find something singular and dramatic a person does, instead of just gluing on a label that limits meaning to present-day fashion and won't make sense fifty years hence.

Take data about a speaker's age and size. "Standing under the orange hoop, I was the only freshman who could lift one ape-long arm and brush net." This says age and size and basketball prowess while being evocative. "I tried to hunch inside the new letter jacket, but my bony wrists stuck out." This adds an element of psychology—self-consciousness.

Rather than simply describing his father's physique in *Angela's Ashes*, Frank McCourt dispenses data about the price on his father's head and then occupies a child's mind pondering his father's actual noggin being paid for.

> [My father] fought with the Old IRA and for some desperate act he wound up a fugitive with a price on his head.
>   When I was a child I would look at my father, the thinning hair, the collapsing teeth, and wonder why anybody would give money for a head like that. When I was thirteen my father's mother told me a secret: as a wee lad your poor father was dropped on his head. It was an accident. He was never the same after, and you must remember that people dropped on their heads can be a bit peculiar.

McCourt's talent for verbal wit packed into a child's mindset means the paternal bean serves as an occasion for dispensing other, more dramatic data. He lets us hear in his grandmother's voice how he learned about his father's dropped-on head. This foreshadows the family's coming disasters and promises drama, piquing a reader's curiosity. In the course of all that, he gives us a carnal portrait of the old man, too.

George Orwell's moving memoir of the Spanish Civil War, *Homage to Catalonia*, also palms off key data in a subtle way. Rather than start with the political sects and conflicts within the revolutionary ranks, he focuses on his encounter with a single Italian freedom fighter. The description of the young guy locates the book as a song of praise to the peasant people Orwell futilely fought alongside against fascism. It's one of dozens such portraits, and it shows us why he's there.

> He was a tough-looking youth of twenty-five or -six, with reddish yellow hair and powerful shoulders. His peaked leather cap was pulled fiercely over one eye. He was standing in profile to me, his chin on his breast, gazing with a puzzled frown at a map, which one of the officers had open on the table. Something in the face deeply moved me. It was the face of a man who would commit murder and throw away his life for a friend—the kind of face you would expect in an Anarchist, though likely as not he was a Communist. . . . As we went out he stepped across the room and gripped my hand very hard. Queer the affection you can feel for a stranger! It was as though his spirit and mine had momentarily succeeded in bridging the gulf of language and tradition and meeting in utter intimacy. I hope he liked me as well as I liked him.

By speculating whether he's an Anarchist or a Communist, Orwell lets us in on the dissent within the leftist ranks while saving us the boredom of a lengthy political disquisition. He knows he has to make us care about the people first, so he shares a sliver of how he came to care. What makes Orwell a genius is trusting that this small, strange moment that touched him so deeply could also touch a reader if he told it frankly enough.

In any good memoir, the writer tries to meet the reader where she is by offering information in the way it's felt—to reflect the writer's inner values and cares either in clever linguistic form (like McCourt) or dramatic scene (like Orwell).

14 | Personal Run-Ins with Fake Voices

> *"The difference between mad people and sane people,"*
> *Brave Orchid explained to the children, "is that sane*
> *people have variety when they talk story. Mad people*
> *have only one story that they talk over and over."*
>
> Maxine Hong Kingston, *The Woman Warrior*

As I've detailed elsewhere, it took me fifteen years of scribbling—first in poetry, then in fiction—to dredge up nerve to tell my childhood story in a voice that fit my face. Before then, I hid from readers on pages that sugarcoated any emotional truths about us all, part of an overall effort to sanitize our past and remold myself into somebody smarter, faster, funnier than harsh reality had afforded me to become.

Literature, when I was growing up, had been the stuff of cool, diffident, hypereducated white guys. And I was solidly blue-collar, crown princess of the crap job—crayfish trucker, waitress, T-shirt factory seamstress—a dropout with an itinerant past. In my zip code of origin, I'd hazard that I was the library's most devoted *New Yorker* customer. John Cheever's tales of East Coast swells who drank their Scotch neat won me. They had swimming pools, they used *summer* as a verb, and I wanted to sound like them despite the fact that the only books I identified much with were by writers of color like Maya Angelou. Reading Angelou's first in 1971, it wasn't just *You can write about this?* but *You can write about* us*?* Even though her family was black and mine white, I hewed more to her worldview than to the four-in-hand tie knotters riding the club car or going to the Yale game in Cheever and Salinger and Fitzgerald's books.

During my short college stint, every time I picked up a pen, this grinding, unnamed fear overcame me—later identified as fear that my real self would spill out. One can't mount a stripper pole wearing a metal diving suit. What I needed to write kept simmering up while I wrote down everything but that. In fact, I kept ginning out reasons that writing reality was impossible. I cranked up therapy and drank like a fish.

By twenty-two I was soaking myself in the French poets who'd enthralled T. S. Eliot. At my age, he'd been writing *Prufrock* and studying philosophy at the Sorbonne, which unlike Eliot, I pronounced "the Sore Bone." Also unlike him, I read these guys in translation. From biographies of Arthur Rimbaud and Charles Baudelaire, I tried to fashion an outlaw poet mask. I wore black clothes and scarlet lipstick and borrowed Mother's old beret.

I scribbled languid, vague poems about Paris—a place I'd barely been—and a man I'd left there but barely remembered. And those young poems of mine were sequined and embroidered with classical references to writers I'd hardly read—the Cynic Diogenes, whose motto, "Live like a dog," fitted (I thought) my faux-punk Patti Smith facade.

What did I write about? Wanting to get laid, not getting laid, getting laid badly. Wanting a guy to leave, wanting a guy not to leave. Then he leaves. In a persona poem, an old gambler makes stiff statements about the nature of chance à la Stéphane Mallarmé's "Throw of the Dice." (Daddy had often gone out to shoot craps when we'd needed money for school clothes.)

Try to find a poet whose talent differed from mine more than Eliot—tight as a rolled umbrella, somebody once called him—or insurance executive Wallace Stevens or prim Miss Dickinson. It'd be hard. They're poets known for experimental bents and hermetic symbolic systems that can forge intense psychological spaces in a reader's head. Their voices also tend toward the reticent. In a similar vein was New York School wizard John Ashbery, a glib, easeful, prolific god whose cool stream of consciousness I worshiped. My critical thesis on him topped a hundred pages—this on a poet who admits he's indecipherable and cares not one whit if the reader gets him. This whole herd of poets—all but Dickinson classically educated—operates on elision and emotional reserve.

By contrast, I was a feral American half aborigine, drinking and pogoing around rock clubs while hotly suffering my disintegrating, hard-drinking, well-armed family.

During this time, my idea of fessing up was to obscure any actual memory and siphon all feeling off till there was naught but sawdust on the page. "Tell the truth but tell it slant," Dickinson had said, not "Drape gauze all over it so it can't be seen." There's a difference between mystery and obscurity, poet Donald Justice once said. About real mystery—Hilary Mantel's run-ins with ghosts, say—a writer can say every dang thing she knows without lessening the enigma's power; obscurity is just hiding out of cowardice what fundamentally needs unveiling.

Here's an execrable excerpt from my 1978 poem "Civiliza-
tion and Its Discontents"—a pretentious reference to Freud's
masterpiece. It was my way of writing about Mother's break-
down, during which she'd set fire to our toys and menaced us
with butcher knife raised.

> In 1959 some doctors sedated
> a Texas housewife, fastened electrodes to her
> temples and flipped on the current. Her hair,
> singed, curled loosely around her eyes
> which are pale green and dumb in the photo
> of her release. This
> is where the story ends for the housewife
> who had once danced flamenco in a bowling alley.
> It's hard to say how much of her
> daughter burned away. She evaporated
> into puberty and gin and became
> a victim of rumor.

I won't bother to say what all is wrong with this—the snotty,
devil-may-care tone, which would better fit a jokester fool like
Letterman; or the crap line breaks—violent enjambments and
uneven syllabic pattern chosen for no reason. There's no data
about who the woman is or why you should care. Plus it's in
no way true. Mother never danced flamenco in a bowling alley.
Nobody ever did or would—a fine example of my limited fictional imagination. Puberty and gin mean nothing—they're
a gesture. About what? Who knows? How postpubescent and
hard-drinking and world-weary I was?

Mother did way more interesting stuff. When she adjudged
the small-town supermarket's Parmesan unworthy, she up-
ended the whole cheese display. She wagged a shotgun at the
ice cream truck when its bells woke her from a nap. She owned

a couture suit from Paris and gave me Sartre's *Nausea* to read when I was in sixth grade.

But I was somehow stifled from speaking directly about the far-more-interesting facts, much less the events that ran through my nightmares and kept me dragging to a shrink's office.

If I wrote vaguely enough, I risked nothing. No one could understand what was going on. I once heard a quote by Marvin Bell on his early work: "I knew I was an experimental poet. My poems didn't make sense."

In a private workshop with Etheridge Knight—an ex-con from Mississippi and elsewhere, ashy of knee and with hands rusty enough to strike a match on—he scolded me about the pretentious pages I turned in. Way before poetry slams, he used to take us into bars or onto crowded buses to read out loud. Facing a listing drunk or a footsore commuter, you figure out pretty quick how irrelevant much of your drivel is.

During this time, my much-loved old man was killing himself with drink. And the one poem Etheridge kinda liked of mine was about a suicidal dog. (The first line was "Don't do it, Dog.") That jokey riff was as close as I could come to the deep mourning that corroded my insides like battery acid as I drove Etheridge crazy with my evasions, spiraling around the home-based subjects haunting me.

In a poem called "Invisible Man," I actually faked both being black and knowing about scientific notions of entropy. In another called "The Double Helix," I quacked on about genetics, a subject that I only knew existed through the similarly titled memoir by Francis Crick and James D. Watson.

Then I had a lightning stroke of luck. I blindly bumbled

into one of the planet's best conversations about memoir. Age twenty-three, loose as a hard-slammed Ping-Pong ball, I found myself rolling into a graduate program in poetry—the only one that would take me sans college diploma, and then only on probation till I proved I wasn't as dumb as I looked (which I probably couldn't have been).

I remember the room and the gray metal chair from which I first heard Geoffrey Wolff read about his con-man father. It was August in Vermont, and hot. Somebody turned off the gale-force floor fan as he stepped to the light wood podium so we could hear him better.

With his Hemingway beard and polo shirt, Geoffrey looked like he'd be equally at home propping up a martini glass in some smoky jazz dive or on a Cuban swordfish boat. His wife was an elegant woman whose opinions people cared about. A Princeton grad who wrote for *Esquire* and the *Washington Post*, Geoffrey had all the credentials you'd need, but he wore them lightly. He was handsome and hearty, but he brooked no shit and seemed worried about nothing more than getting words down in the right order. At parties he dispensed pricey cognac, told riveting stories, and talked about jazz.

The summer of 1978, the stuffy room he was reading in held fewer than a hundred exhausted, mostly young writers and their not-yet-forty-year-old professors.

But the minute he started to read, a fine current sizzled through the air. People who'd been slumped in their chairs—mentors and tormentors mostly exhausted from a day spent poring over our medium-shitty pages—straightened up. We leaned forward. The occasional fly buzz became audible.

Geoffrey had a strong voice, but he read from the book haltingly. It hurt him to read, you could tell. He plowed on, though, stopping sometimes to drink water, and nobody shifted. Hell, I hardly blinked. He was showing me a form of courage I knew I didn't have. He was like some action-movie hero gunning down the enemy I'd faced my whole life—family lies—with such panache I couldn't feature not enlisting. It was a heroic performance. And I wanted nothing so much as to have the balls to do the same with my own story. The audience exploded clapping after.

And what an audience. There was the herd of poets I'd been busily padding around behind like a puppy. (Name-drop alert: Louise Glück, Heather McHugh, Robert Hass, Ellen Bryant Voigt—even Charles Simić visited.) They all wrote psychologically sharp stuff drawn in varying degrees of transparency from their own life events. On the prose side was Ray Carver, whose first paperback I'd lugged around Europe the year before, as well as Richard Ford and Marilynne Robinson.

Geoffrey's brother Toby was there. He hadn't yet written *This Boy's Life*, but alongside him sat Frank Conroy, whose *Stop-Time* was a cult classic excerpted in the *New Yorker*, where it showed up as fiction. With those teachers at hand, it's small wonder that chums Mark Doty and Jerry Stahl would join me in writing memoir.

After grad school, I vanished into a job in the telecommunications business, writing at night and publishing as I could, but my poems strayed as far from my natural abilities as I could steer them.

On my thirtieth birthday, I flew back from a San Francisco business trip on the red-eye to Boston—a flight briefly aborted by a bomb scare. This afforded me some bar time. I spent every bit of change I could rifle from my cheap briefcase before I sloshed aboard, then pounded the champagne they doled out clear back to Boston. It was a dark time in my family—when wasn't it? I couldn't forget the specter of my shriveling daddy in a Texas nursing home. He'd be dead within the year, and part of me knew it.

The red-eye flew east toward the arcing sun. And all night, across the spiral notebook, my hand hardly stopped moving. A great, mournful cry poured out, page after page. I gripped the pen so hard my thumb hurt when I got off at dawn.

Once home, I emptied my briefcase, slapping the notebook on the kitchen counter. Then I set off for the mind-numbing task of faking a business career. Had I been scrawling all night on loose paper, I'd have tossed what I'd written in the trash. That's how wretched I figured it was.

Later, my husband bent over the pages. A reserved guy, he had a keen look. "I was wondering when you'd get around to writing this," he said.

The thought of him eying those raw, unfiltered pages embarrassed me. Few opinions mattered more than his—he was brilliant, ruthless, and didn't truck in flattery. And he liked what I'd set down. He was one of the many fine writers—including all my teachers—telling me the pages came alive when I wrote in first person. It somehow felt small or weak or whiny to me.

Still, at his urging and reurging, I took the pages and started to cannibalize them for lines and language and tone. Out came a few elegies and other poems both lyric and narrative, along with some hunks of prose that would wind up in *Liars' Club*.

Here's one excerpt about my old man. It's better than anything I'd done before. But it still sounded so emotionally bald that I only sent it out to a magazine at my husband's urging.

> I tell the only truth I know:
> that I am helpless and sorry you're dying,
> that this planet will weigh no less when you
> are ash. . . .
> and if, as Buddha says, life and death are illusory
> I will be fooled and suffer your absence,
> and somewhere you'll always be
> rising from your oxygen tent, a modern Lazarus,
> or snapping open a Lone Star beer,
> or simply, too tired to talk, scraping mud
> from your black work boots onto the porch.

The great Latin rhetoricians advised orators that funeral speeches should be unadorned, free of flowery similes without a lot of embroidery, but at the time these words—which don't seem so awful now—seemed shamefully simple, hardly the stuff of capital-L Literature.

Plus I had more posturing to do. The next line has Wittgenstein in it—dragged in, as Etheridge might have said, kicking and screaming.

> And if, as Wittgenstein thinks, problems are grammatical,
> I confess I find no syntax to pull
> nails from a coffin . . .

Good Lord, I now think. The subject matter was bubbling up in me to be written, but I was yammering about Wittgenstein.

It strikes me now as twee to call "Father" the man who'd never been anything but Daddy. Too Sylvia Plath to call him Daddy, I figured.

In Cambridge in those years, fiction seemed the grand form women aspired to. Almost all the women I admired—Toni Morrison, Mona Simpson, Alice Walker, Sue Miller, Susan Minot, Alice Munro, Tillie Olsen, Joyce Carol Oates, Marilynne Robinson, Amy Tan—were working in fiction. And so I started a novel. What the hell did I know about fiction? Only that it permitted masquerade.

So what all did I change from reality?

First, I made myself an only child. That'd teach my country-club sister to throw me out of her mansion! Second, instead of my sloppy, paint-splattering drunk mother, the mom's a ballerina—sylph-like, disciplined, bun-headed. Third, the narrator (aka me) is precocious as hell. She's beautiful and noble and wise. She does calculus at twelve and volunteers at the local nursing home. She never bites anybody! Finally, I made sure that we as a family actually functioned like normal.

When a stroke fells the novel's daddy, the mother and daughter stay at the hospital overnight, sleeping on chairs. On the actual night, we'd left him for Mother's surprise birthday party, where we got drunk on margaritas and I later ran over his cat (not fatally). In fiction, we talk out insurance worries, instead of Mother threatening to shoot herself if I couldn't straighten out her reimbursements. The novel's mom actually consoles the grieving daughter; my mother was more akin to a lackadaisical reptile owner, flicking the terrarium to see if I was still alive.

And here's the tone and voice.

> On my sixteenth birthday, my mother presented
> me a pair of nineteenth-century opera glasses from
> France—gold-plated binoculars small enough to fit in
> a pearl-beaded evening bag. This gift might lead you
> to think that we occupied a different sort of world
> than we did, that we regularly attended some opera
> house, that we climbed in and out of a lot of taxicabs
> as doormen held umbrellas over us.

Even while the novel's first paragraph refutes the opera glasses, claiming they aren't who we are, they start the dang book. And as Freud says, there are no negatives in the unconscious. Even the diction—*presented* instead of *gave*—is a stilted stand-in for the vernacular I'd wind up with.

But the glasses had a source in lived events. Daddy *had* once given me his old army binoculars. Instead of those, this novel's mother somehow delivers an effete, gold-plated doodah that opposes not just Daddy's field glasses but the whole backwater Texas milieu I was actually born to. And not insignificantly, the glasses come from my way-disinterested mother, not my thought-I-hung-the-moon daddy. Holy wish fulfillment, Sigmund.

Meanwhile, I painted my character just as prettily, as in this paragraph, where I do my clichéd double-vision thing of looking through the glasses at the following idyllic scene.

> A cardinal in a chinaberry tree picked at a green
> berry that looked as big as an apple. A dragonfly lit
> on a white cape jasmine flower, its wings whirring
> and shimmering. Chameleons dozed like miniature
> dinosaurs on tree twigs.

I managed to find something pretty to blot out the rough, industrial landscape I grew up in, which was famously ugly, run through by snakes and alligators and mosquito hordes. How did I restrain myself from putting in the little Irish guy with a green derby from the Lucky Charms commercial? In truth, the only time I was involved in nature at all was toting a shotgun to murder an animal.

What's wrong with this as writing? I interact with no one. There's no action, no story. I don't seem to want anything other than to pose adorably with a lorgnette from the Lincoln administration.

But isn't this using my strength? Poets are good at describing stuff, right? Shouldn't I do that as much as possible? Yes, but unless the description helps the story along or reveals something psychological, it's froufrou, embroidery, decor.

In 1991, after five years, I delivered the novel to my hard-drinking, hell-for-leather writer's group, which was famous for making people cry. I still have longhand notes from Sven Birkerts and Robert Polito (was Lewis Hyde there?). They patiently say: "Try this as memoir." "Your essays are good, maybe do this as nonfiction." "TRIM!!"

Looking back, every arrow aimed at a throbbing neon sign that read *memoir*. As Elizabeth Hardwick told Robert Lowell before he invented confessional poetry, "Why not just say what happened."

The voice I'd eventually figure for that first memoir drew from a lifetime of reading, which my mother had fostered. An artist and history maven, she kept a wobbly tower of books by her bed. She was smart and witty—master of the one-liner—but not much of a storyteller.

The talk of my barroom aficionado daddy ran rich with figurative language. If a woman had an ample backside, he might say, "She had a butt like two bulldogs fighting in a bag," which—believe it or not—was a positive attribute.

Instead of milking this current running naturally through my head, I'd tried in my novel to sound like some fluffy, ruffly Little Bo Peep.

Daddy's manner of speaking would unlock the book for me. Daddy, the in-house exile in our household of book-reading females, would solve my biggest literary problem. He was a legendary storyteller in the bars and gambling joints across our county. For an anthro class in college, I'd even recorded some of his tales. But his manner of talk was so singular, I didn't need to listen to the tapes. The stories hummed through my fibers.

It's ironic that the very redneckese I'd spent some time trying to rise above wound up branding my work like hot iron on a steer's ass. Without borrowing from Daddy's voice—without the grit and grime of where I'd grown up—I'd been playing with one hand tied back.

When there was a thunderstorm, Daddy might say, "It's raining like a cow pissing on a flat rock," which, for all purposes, is a line of poetry. The crisp image jolts a little. It yanks you out of the quotidian. It operates just beyond the bounds of propriety, as poems should. Plus, the minute you laugh at it, you become loosely complicit in the speaker's offensive speech. This binds you to the narrator. You've bought in. (The same kind of buy-in happens in any superfantastic premise—think George Saunders's story "Fox 8," where the minute you accept the premise that a fox is writing, you've sort of been psychically hijacked by the narrator. He owns your belief system.)

That single line also evokes an entirely new world in which cows piss on flat rocks and folks stand around to marvel at it.

Metaphors helped to flesh out experiences and texture the language as my father talked. The wind came through boxcar cracks during the Depression "like a straight razor."

He had a talent for physical detail and a bemused attention to the human comedy. Until drink ate him up, he was a keen observer, with a knack for zeroing in on a luminous image. At a random stoplight, he'd laugh like hell just seeing a big fat guy on a moped with its tires squashed down. He liked marbled meat and unfiltered Camels; he ate onions raw. He argued from external evidence—a fully imagined place—and the slapstick and violence of his tales drew you in mostly through the vivid portrayals a carnal person has a knack for.

But most of all, Daddy loved his characters. There were buffoons, sure, but affection shone through every tale. Unlike a lot of other barroom show-offs I've listened to, he had to be coaxed into talking, and his stories never seemed designed to punk anybody. He frequently made fun of his own lunkheaded antics, as when his brothers convinced him at a fair to get in the boxing ring with a kangaroo, who quite literally kicked his ass. I hoped his attitude of fond humility would underpin my own vision.

However much I borrowed from Daddy's language and attitude, I knew any voice authentic to my youth would have to accommodate the hours I spent pinched and wondering in my head. My inner life sometimes felt bigger than my exterior—it's just how I'm wired, I guess. So my voice couldn't just mimic his. I had all manner of stuff to talk about that he'd roll his eyes at. Literary references and therapy were just two. But to package those in idiom was to keep the voice consistent, and to admit my posturing as I went:

I was in my twenties . . . and liked to call myself a
poet and had affected a habit of reading classical texts
(in translation, of course—I was a lazy student). . . .
[I'd] spend days dressed in black in the scalding heat
of my mother's front porch reading Homer (or Ovid
or Virgil) and waiting for somebody to ask me what I
was reading. No one ever did. People asked me what
I was drinking, how much I weighed, where I was
living, and if I'd married yet, but no one gave me a
chance to deliver my lecture on Great Literature.

The aforementioned bullshit opera glasses I'd started with
in fiction finally became what they'd been to start with in fact:
army-issue field binoculars, written in below, in a voice much
more alive in time and place and with shame and malice and
an anecdote and a sense of place:

I stepped through the back screen and held [the field
glasses] up to my eyes. Through our fence slats, I
could make out Mickey Heinz sitting on his fat knees
next door, running his dump truck through the dirt. I
could never see Mickey without a wince. I'd once
gotten him to smoke Nestle's Quik we'd rolled up in
toilet paper. . . . He'd blistered [his tongue] so bad he'd
run to show his mother, not considering how she and
all his people belonged to one of those no-smoking,
no-dancing churches. Mrs. Heinz whapped his butt
bad with a hairbrush. We listened to the whole thing
squatting right underneath the Heinz bathroom
window—the whap-whap of that plastic brush on
Mickey's blubbery little ass, him howling like a
banshee. . . . I was longing for Daddy's truck to lunge
into the garage.

This scene—rendered truly as I could make it—comes in the language of the kid I was at the time. It has some character data inside it: that I handled my own bad feelings by picking on Mickey Heinz, but felt somewhat bad about it, at least. Plus I am situated later among other kids, who pose dramatic possibilities for me later. The scene includes some inner life, an anecdote, and finally Daddy shows up at its end.

I spent nine hard, exasperating, concentrated months on the first chapter of *Liars' Club* alone, which was essentially time developing that voice—a watchmaker's minuscule efforts, noodling with syntax and diction. Were I to add on the time I spent trying to recount that book's events in poetry and a novel, I could argue that concocting that mode of speech actually occupied some thirteen years (seventeen, if you count the requisite years in therapy getting the nerve up). What was I doing during those nine months? Mostly I just shoved words around the page. I'd get up at four or five when my son was asleep, then work. I'd try telling something one way, then another. If a paragraph seemed half decent, I'd cut it out and tape it to the wall.

The voice had to be consistent to sound true. Tone could vary, but diction and syntax had to match up. A reader had to believe the same person was speaking throughout—this is an apparatus, of course. Listen to anybody all the time, and the mode of speech shifts around. Mostly assembling the voice was intuitive, but I did find some minor rules for my narrator to stick with, even if "naturally" I'd speak a whole lot of other ways.

Like, I consciously ended sentences on prepositions. "There

was a lifeguard whose bathing suit we spent half the summer looking up the leg hole of." This is idiomatic and oral. It scorns formal grammar. You can't have one sentence that way, then warp the syntax around in the next paragraph to sound "correct." To wit:

> *It was the same yellow door we'd gone through*
> is a different critter speaking than one who says
> *It was the yellow door through which we had gone.*

The diction had to be consistent too. So I kept calling my Mother *Mother*—not Mama, sometimes, then Mommy, then Mom, whether "that's how it really happened" or not. Changing what I called her would signal some psychological shift, which I'd have to stop and explain. I just picked *Mother* and stuck with it.

It's a cliché to talk about *finding* a voice, but it does feel arrived at, fixed and immutable as the angel hidden in Michelangelo's stone. About nine months into working on the first chapter for a proposal (I'd been told I needed a hundred pages and an outline), I started knowing where the words went. Plus an obvious order rose up—mostly chronological, with one flash forward at the outset.

It didn't happen in one instant. But over a period of a few days I went through a profound psychological shift. The images in my head suddenly had words representing them on the page. And accompanying the words was a state of consciousness. It almost felt like I'd walked into some inner room where my lived experiences could pass through and come out as language.

If the voice worked as a living contract with the reader, it also strangely bound me to candor. To make stuff up would somehow have broken the spell the voice cast over me. Even fake names slid some glass down between me and the past. I had to do the whole book with real names and descriptions and do global find/replace afterward. Odd, that.

Whatever the source of the voice—self-hypnosis, psychological peace, the ghost of Papa Hem saying *Write one true sentence*, or the Lord God on high—its arrival changed the whole game. I honestly don't know if a shift in mind predated the voice or vice versa. But suddenly I felt the wagon I'd been pulling like a trudging ox was a vehicle with an engine, moving down the road. Pages started piling up. And two and a half years later I had a full draft of what went into print—so close they set type by it.

15 | On Book Structure and the Order of Information

Do you wish to be great? Then begin by being. Do you desire to create a vast and lofty fabric? Think first about the foundations of humility. The higher your structure is to be, the deeper must be its foundation.

St. Augustine, *City of God*

In terms of basic book shape, I've used the same approach in all three of mine: I start with a flash forward that shows what's at stake emotionally for me over the course of a book, then tell the story in straightforward, linear time.

I wouldn't suggest that shape for everybody, but I would say you have to start out setting emotional stakes—why the enterprise is a passionate one for you, what's at risk—early on. That's why the flashback structure, which I borrowed from Conroy and Crews (among thousands of other storytellers), is a time-honored one. It's sitting on the coffin, telling the tale of a death—or rebirth, in my case.

Young writers often ask me to help them order information in a story. But there's a proven method you can try. Imagine sitting down to tell it to a pal at lunch. You'd have no problem figuring out what goes where.

Usually the big story seems simple: *They were assholes, I was a saint.* If you look at it ruthlessly, you may find the story was more like: *I richly provoked them, and they became assholes*; or, *They were mostly assholes, but could be a lot of fun to be with*; or, *They were so sick and sad, they couldn't help being assholes, the poor bastards*; or, *We took turns being assholes.* . . . (I always joke to students that everything I've ever written started out: *I am sad. The end. By Mary Karr.*)

There's the big, almost-capital-S Story of a whole book (how I survived becoming an orphan by hiking the Pacific Crest Trail, say), and there are smaller stories or anecdotes—the time Stooge and I stole the watermelons. If you let yourself tell those smaller anecdotes or stories, the overarching capital-S Story will eventually rise into view.

16 | The Road to Hell Is Paved with Exaggeration

don't brandish your stump
over other people's heads
don't knock your white cane
on the panes of the well-fed

Zbigniew Herbert,
"Mr. Cogito Reflects on Suffering"

To hammer home for practitioners what I've said before, the worst events or the most spectacular wins don't make the best books. Maybe the most truly felt event does—or some cunning mix of voice and story shaped by passion. Plenty of folks have triumphed over way more than I ever faced. I was born in the richest country in the world to literate, employed parents who owned their home. Some start out brain-damaged in rape camps in far-flung gulags. My suffering is not one iota of what such folks endure.

To manufacture stuff in hopes of selling more books means you never do honor to your own trials and conquests, what Faulkner might call your postage stamp of reality. If you trust that what you felt deeply warrants your emotional response, try to honor your past by writing it that way. Sometimes true agony is not even discernible to the human eye. As a kid, when I saw my mother's mouth become a straight line and heard her speak in a Yankee accent as her posture went super straight, I knew she was tanked. The rat scrabble this set off in my head, as I tried to figure out how to stop the chaos approaching us like a runaway train, was torment. Rendering a small external stimulus inside a child's impotent body can provide a moving experience for a reader.

Also, making you and yours seem hyperbizarre can keep a reader from identifying with you or being inside an experience.

Some writers' talents work in the realm of the hyperbizarre, but they're rare. My abilities seem more tethered to the real rather than the surreal, so I try to normalize the strange so the reader can access it.

17 | Blind Spots and False Selves

*We apply certain kinds of pressure to you, under which
you are forced to flee to your highest ground. . . . But
hopefully, under that pressure, you leave behind all of
the false You's—the imitative You, the too-clever You,
the Avoiding You—and settle into that (sometimes, at
first, disappointing) beast, Real You. . . . Real You is all
you have, and all other paths are false. And in the best
case, Real You is so happy to finally be recognized, it
rewards you with Originality.*

George Saunders,
MFA graduation speech, Syracuse University, 2013

In memoir the heart is the brain. It's the Geiger counter you run
over memory's landscape looking for precious metals to light up.
A psychological self-awareness and faith in the power of truth
gives you courage to reveal whatever you unearth, whether you
come out looking vain or conniving or hateful or not.

Any memoirist's false selves (plural) will take turns plaster-
ing themselves across his real mouth to silence the scarier fact
of who he is. Writing as directly as possible out of that single
"true" core and nascent ability will naturally unify pages. Otherwise, there will be inconsistencies that read as fake.

False choices based on who you wish you were will result
in places where the voice goes awry or the details chosen ring
false. If Helen Keller wrote from the viewpoint of a nearsighted
girl rather than a blind one or if Maya Angelou made herself

an orphaned paraplegic or a light-skinned black girl who could pass in the Jim Crow South . . . well, you can see how their stories would've been bled of raw power.

Many of the truths a memoirist starts out believing morph into something wholly other. Again: anybody maladroit at apology or changing her mind just isn't bent for the fluid psychological state that makes truth discoverable.

You think you know the story so well. It's a mansion inside your head, each room just waiting to be described, but pretty much every memoirist I've ever talked to finds the walls of such rooms changing shape around her. There are shattering earthquakes, tectonic-plate-type shifts. Or it's like memory is a snow globe that invariably gets shaken so as to shroud the events inside.

Geoffrey Wolff claimed he, over the years, inadvertently shaped his old man into a more dashing, gangsteresque figure than he'd been:

> It had always been convenient to see my Father in melodramatic terms, as extraordinarily seedy or criminal. But the things I'd dined out on weren't emotionally accurate.

Before writing his Vietnam memoir, Tobias Wolff discovered that the letters he'd sent his mother—which he'd remembered as soft-focus, composed to shield her from fret—actually ramped up the danger he'd faced.

When Gary Shteyngart worked on his mesmerizing *Little Failure*, he came to realize what a dutiful son he'd in fact always been. Family lore held he was an ingrate and a bounder who cost his parents no end of misery.

Of course, revelations come to anybody who prods around in the past, memoirist or not. Ten years before my first book, I confronted my mother about why Daddy, who'd stoically tolerated her tantrums and wagging firearms at him, had stayed with her. She'd said, "He felt sorry for me." The instant she said it, I knew it for truth, and yet it overturned a lifetime of believing she'd held all the power in their marriage. His silence hadn't been helplessness—it hadn't even been love. It had been pity.

Mostly we get in trouble when we start trying to unpack those sound bites I mentioned. Ideas that hold decades of interpretation can lie to us worst of all: *I was tough, I was beleaguered, I was ugly.* In Shteyngart's *Little Failure*, his parents called him ugly so often, I was astonished to find plastered across the published work's cover (having read an early manuscript) a snapshot of the slim, darkly handsome, long-lashed boy. He was solemn enough to rival the young hemophiliac czar-to-be! Hell, who wouldn't look solemn when called ugly so often? Of course, for the purposes of memoir, it matters not whether he was perceptibly ugly, only that he felt so.

No matter how much you're gunning for truth, the human ego is also a stealthy, low-crawling bastard, and for pretty much everybody, getting used to who you are is a lifelong spiritual struggle. Start trying to bring yourself to the page, and fear of how you'll come off besets even the most forthright. The best you can hope for is to rip off each mask as you find it blotting out your vision.

· · ·

We each nurture a private terror that some core aspect(s) of either our selves or our story must be hidden or disowned. With every manuscript I've ever edited—even grown-assed writers'—the traits a writer often fights hardest to hide may serve as undeniable facets both of self and story. You bumble onto scenes that blow up fond notions of the past, or whole shifts in attitude practically rewrite you where you stand.

In even great writers' books, you'll find whole chapters worth skipping because they feel like emotional detours. They're included because the writer has some shiny aspect of the self that the chapter polishes to high sheen. Nabokov devotes the third chapter of *Speak, Memory* to all his family estates and heraldry and his fancy-pants ancestors, Baron von So-and-So and Count Suck-On-This. It's stuff he's secretly proud of, without ever admitting as much. But here's how dull the writing gets inside that small, understandable vanity:

> Two other, much more distant, estates in the region were related to Batovo: my uncle Prince Wittgenstein's Druzhnoselie situated a few miles beyond the Siverski railway station, which was six miles northeast of our place.

He's preening, in a way. Eventually he also casually drops how Uncle Ruka left him a couple million dollars in 1916. And he claims he has no long grouse against the Soviet dictatorship for having made off with this rightful inheritance. But he argues this disinterest in cash so hard, I have a hard time swallowing it.

> The following passage is not for the general reader, but for the particular idiot who, because he lost a

> fortune in some crash, thinks he understands me. . . .
> The nostalgia I have been cherishing all these years
> is a hypertrophied sense of lost childhood, not sorrow
> for lost banknotes.

Point being: it would feel more honest to this reader if he confessed to begrudging the lost cash—who wouldn't? At this chapter's end he gets back to a beautiful reverie. It's somewhat reassuring that even a masterpiece like *Speak, Memory* sags a little with the weight of one chapter, where we sense that Nabokov is showing off his exotic pedigree without admitting as much. Mary McCarthy perpetrates a similar gaffe in *Catholic Girlhood*, devoting a chapter to her role in a school play and her mastery of Latin in a way that points up her cleverness. Students always rankle against that chapter. Ditto Hemingway, who in *A Moveable Feast* (1964) seems to be slyly mocking Fitzgerald when he chooses to recount a talk they allegedly had about F. Scott's penis size.

Somebody once asked me if I minded the review that claimed I was too circumspect in describing my son's father in *Lit*, so he comes off two-dimensional as any WASP in an L.L.Bean catalog. My answer? If I'd written it better, it would've worked for every reader. Writing about him had tormented me, and those passages did feel weaker than the rest.

Another divorce failure, I think, occurs in Elizabeth Gilbert's much-adored *Eat, Pray, Love*, which otherwise displays a nice mix of circumspection and candor. She overtly blames herself for the demise of her marriage, for instance, and for not wanting to have a baby. She claims the reasons for the divorce are too private—drawing a curtain I respect across those events without seeming coy.

But right after, she mulls over at considerable length the dickering details of her husband's settlement. Is that not too private? She first offers to sell everything, and then to split it fifty-fifty. "What if he took all the assets and I took all the blame?"

> [He] was also asking for things I never even considered (a stake in the royalties of books I'd written during the marriage, a cut of possible future movie rights to my work, a share of my retirement accounts). . . . It would cost me dearly, but a fight in the courts would be infinitely more expensive and time-consuming, not to mention soul-corroding.

Now divorce writing may be the toughest thing a memoirist can do other than covering a war, nor could I render my own any better. But while she takes the time to detail all her ex's unfair requests, she never lets us in on the source of what seems like buckets of money for a New York freelance writer. She sports an apartment, a house in the 'burbs, a retirement account. She flies a friend along on her book tour for company. Even a simple "I'd come into some money" or "Movie rights made me flush" would help. This is a minor bump in the book's long journey, but it proves that even the most successful of us misstep from time to time, showing what we should hide and hiding what the reader needs.

We more often fail by omitting key scenes. Cheryl Strayed was almost done with *Wild* when she discovered two incidents that—once you've read her story—seem so psychologically crucial you can't believe they'd ever been passed over.

The first involves how she and her teenage brother have to

shoot their dead mother's horse. Before Strayed's hiking trip, her beloved mother dies a swift and agonizing death of cancer, leaving behind an ancient, broken-down nag named Lady. Strayed's stepfather—once an amazing dad—has, after her mother has passed, gotten over it pretty fast, even moving a new girlfriend into Strayed's childhood house. He promises to have the animal put down by a vet.

He's away on Christmas Eve when Cheryl and her brother—she twenty, he eighteen—come back to the homestead for the last time to find the bony animal shivering in a snowfield. She spoke to me about it recently on the phone:

> My heart was shredded. The closest we could come to killing my mother was killing that horse, which was like her god.

It's a wrenching scene: "The bullet hit Lady right between the eyes, in the middle of her white star." After, the kids leave her for coyotes to drag away.

What's captivating to me as a writer is how the memory came to her in a flash. She was driving her kids home from school, not thinking much about the memoir, when she experienced a brief moment of desolation. You know the feeling: a sagging sadness out of nowhere just waylaid her. And that feeling conjured the image of those two kids in the cold, shooting that animal.

It's not like she'd forgotten the event—just overlooked it. Who wants to show up in a book shooting an animal, after all—even if it's a mercy killing? But of course she knew it belonged right off. "I'd been trying to figure out what scenes would show how totally my stepfather had bailed on us," she said. Of course, she only needed that one.

The other memory also involves her stepfather. Toward the end of her thousands-mile-long hike, she's staring into the fire, recalling how her stepfather had taught her to build a fire and pitch a tent.

> From him, I'd learned how to open a can with a jackknife and paddle a canoe and skip a rock on the surface of a lake. . . . But I was pretty certain as I sat there that night that if it hadn't been for Eddie, I wouldn't have found myself on [the trail]. . . . He hadn't loved me well in the end, but he had loved me well when it mattered.

So despite her heartbreak at his leaving, and "though it was true everything I felt for him sat like a boulder in my throat," her load was lightened by all he'd taught her that she could use. She wound up feeling he and her mother had given her all the tools she needed to make it.

Maybe it takes a lifetime to get used to occupying your own body, writer or no. Self-deceit is the bacterium affecting every psyche to varying degrees, especially in youth. We like to view ourselves a certain way. After warning my high school sweetheart—a rock guitarist and music producer whose nickname back then was Little Hendrix—that he might make a cameo in a book about our teen years, he asked, Could I please not mention all the pot we'd smoked as kids? I looked at him, with his mass of hair and slim-fit jeans and boots, and asked him who he thought he was fooling.

In my experience, young writers may stumble early on by

misunderstanding the basic nature of their talents. We want to be who we're not. The badass wants to be a saint, the saint a slut, the slut an intellectual in pince-nez glasses.

My Syracuse colleague George Saunders murdered himself in grad school trying to sound like gritty, working-class minimalist Ray Carver. Ray was a lumbering trailer-park aficionado who favored stark realism using the fewest words, so George showed up driving a beater pickup and sporting a cowboy hat. Forget that he was actually a handsome surfer-looking guy, son of a successful businessman, prom king in his high school. Plus the nature of his talent—which produced for us fantastic talking foxes and cavemen in museum tableaux and masks that permit babies to speak—stands worlds away from Carver's. George's surreal situations grow more from the mode of, say, Isaac Babel or Nikolai Gogol. George trying to be Ray Carver would be like Gabriel García Márquez trying to be Hemingway. One of George's teachers kept trying to steer him back to his humor pieces, which George found "too goofy": "They were just stupid jokes I put in, messing around." But eventually, as he got older, the satirical stuff started to make its way onto the page.

Writing the real self seldom seems original enough when you first happen on it. In fact, usually it growls like a beast and stinks of something rotten. Age and practice help you to rout out vanities after you've ruined perfectly good paper setting them down, but you can't keep them from clotting up early drafts.

And every memoirist I know has a comparable story. I have dozens.

Even this book tricked me. You'd think—after three memoirs and thirty years of teaching—I'd have inoculated myself against posing as somebody other than this damn self I'm stuck with.

But the same deluded fear interferes at some point with pretty much every book I write.

Before starting this, my editor suggested right off keeping it simple, modeling the book on my Syracuse syllabus. But I argued that I was going to elevate the memoir form by following T. S. Eliot's model in his essays or James Wood's in *Broken Estate* or young Elif Batuman's brilliant tome on Russian lit.

Yet those three role models couldn't be further from who I am. They're Ivy Leaguers, lauded intellectuals, fluent in languages and philosophy, leaking IQ points from every pore. I am a backwoods storyteller who's made a living with street vernacular. As if.

Can you guess what my fear is? What kept me generating diddly squat on this very text for months?

That I lack the credentials to write anything with authority. Reared in the Ringworm Belt, I am a dropout. The grad program I went to folded the day after I got my MFA. And yet I planned this book as a work of aesthetics and literary history and phenomenology and neurobiology and yahditah yahditah blah blah.

And this is the self-consciousness that haunts every book! You'd think I could spy the wrong road without first traveling halfway down it. You'd think I could—after decades of tricking myself over the same fear—head off the pretentious bustling that precedes my writing anything and always winds up in the trash.

And yet writing has never been linear for me. I always circle my own stories, avoiding the truth like a pooch staked to a clothesline pole, spiraling closer and closer with each revision till—with each book—my false self finally lines up eye to eye with the true one.

I threw away over 1,200 finished pages of my last memoir and broke the delete key on my keyboard changing my mind. If I had any balls at all, I'd make a brooch out of it.

18 | Truth Hunger: The Public and Private Burning of Kathryn Harrison

Lying is done with words, but also with silence.

Adrienne Rich,
"Women and Honor: Some Notes on Lying"

It takes an obsessive streak that borders on lunacy to go rummaging around in the past as memoirists are wont to do, particularly a fragmented or incendiary past, in which facts are sparse and stories don't match up. I don't know if memoirists as children are lied to more often as kids or only grow up to resent it more, but it does seem we often come from the ranks of orphans or half-orphans-through-divorce, trying to heal schisms inside ourselves. Like everybody, I suppose, people we loved broke our hearts because only they had access to them, and we broke our own hearts later by following their footsteps and reenacting their mistakes.

This earmark of a memoirist no doubt applies to every human being on the planet. But many of us undertake exploring the past precisely because it is so foggy and tenuous in its truths.

Or maybe memoirists' families and platoons and empires actually did blow apart more spectacularly than their less-scarred or less-likely-to-write-about-it counterparts. But being an orphan oddly frees you to speculate and wallow around in memoryville without any correction from outside. The minute our non-memoir-writing counterparts start wondering aloud about this or that event in the past, the memory police—either a tidy matriarch with a chronological photo album or somebody at the VFW—rushes in to say, "That's not how it happened." (Robert Graves was in the same regiment as poet Siegfried Sassoon, and in the latter's copy of *Good-Bye to All That* in the New York Public Library sit marginal notes arguing the veracity of many points Graves made.)

In my house, say, the recording angels stopped regularly filling photo albums when I was about four. Certificates of divorce and marriage and death never got saved. It's all rumor and guesswork.

Mary McCarthy in *Catholic Girlhood* claims losing her parents had broken the chain of "collective memory" that binds the more solvent family. Without a solid history, she and her brother spent a lifetime discussing the past, bent like a pair of bloodhounds to sniff out the old trails. That ongoing dialogue helped to fuel her work for a lifetime before she set pen to paper.

> The very difficulties [of researching our story] have provided an incentive. As orphans, my brother Kevin and I have a burning interest in our past, which we try to reconstruct together, like two amateur archaeologists, falling on any new scrap of evidence, trying to fit it in, questioning our relations, belaboring our own memories. It has been a kind of quest.

Having gone through the profound discomfort of writing from personal history, I don't think most writers amble into this arena to cash in on some grisly past, nor to settle scores, nor to jack up every hangnail into a battlefield amputation. Truth summons them, as it summons the best novelists and poets. And it's not only memoirists who get it wrong. "What is the novelist's sentimentality," Tobias Wolff once said, "—whether expressed in unearned cheer or unearned cynicism—but a lie of the heart." Most memoirists are driven to their projects for their own deeply felt psychological reasons. As Yeats said, "Mad Ireland hurt me into poetry," so most of us have been hurt into memoir.

The memoirists I know don't cleave to veracity so as to keep kinfolks from suing nor to avoid landing on *Oprah* blinking and sweating once they're unmasked. For most, knowing the truth matters more than how they come off telling it. They've spent lifetimes plumbing the past—weighing, questioning, digging around in the old days long after their former companions have sallied forth into tidy forgetfulness or private versions of personal history in which they star as heroes.

Kathryn Harrison was inwardly scalded into writing one of the bravest memoirs in recent memory, only to be blistered by the press for it. (No man I can think of ever took such a public butt-whipping.*) What sin did she commit? In *The Kiss*, she

---

* The year before Harrison's book, Michael Ryan brought out his *Secret Life*, about a sex addiction that drove him to prey on undergrads in his tutelage and even as a kid to boink the family terrier. It received much praise, even landing the cover of the *New York Times Book Review*. War memoirs in which male writers bomb ancestral villages are never reviewed with such character slaughter as Harrison suffered. A man indicted can wind up wildly praised.

breaks a universal cultural taboo—at age twenty, she's seduced by her long-lost preacher father, entering into what she calls an affair with him.

In choosing to digest fully her fractured past, Harrison was possessed of a gnawing hunger for clarity. Because she paid such a high price for exposing said past—the ad hominem attacks on her remain the nastiest I've ever seen—her complex motivations warrant a look.

I posit that her reasons are identical to those of long-venerated memoir masters like Richard Wright, Mary McCarthy, and Vladimir Nabokov—to get the story right.

Like some of us, Harrison at first set out to tell her story in fiction, books she'd later rue as untrue and feel honor-bound to correct. Before *The Kiss*, the subject of incest insinuated itself—"it kept intruding"—into her first three novels. But she particularly hated how, in her first, she located the daughter squarely among the innocent.

> I wrote *The Kiss* in many ways as a response to my
> own first novel, *Thicker Than Water*, which was
> held to be autobiographical. The woman in the story,
> Isabel, has an affair with her father, but Isabel was
> younger than I was at the time. She was more passive,
> sweeter, more of a victim. When I finished that
> book I wanted to disown it. I felt I had betrayed my
> own history. I was dishonest in a way that has been
> inordinately painful to me over the years.

Fiction, rather than bringing events into sharper focus for Harrison, had blurred them further. She was driven to make it right—not squinting-through-your-eyes-looking-through-your-fingers right, but right as only ruthless scrutiny can make it.

She felt fiction had so falsified her tale that "I'd obeyed the cultural silence to keep quiet about incest." So for those who think a writer can flip a switch and go from nonfiction to novel based on social convenience, I've got some bad news. Your psychological proclivity determines which better fits your story. That decision grows from the nature of your character. Autonomy in such choices is a fairy tale.

Of course, fiction can be ruthlessly honest—or it can smear Vaseline on the lens and obscure. A real novelist tells the greater truth with a mask on. I once suggested to Don DeLillo that he write a memoir, and he recoiled. But even black-belt proser Martin Amis undertook his memoir, *Experience*, about his author father, Kingsley Amis, from "a desire to speak, for once, without artifice." For some subjects, fiction won't do. To free herself from the topic as an artist, Harrison turned to memoir. "It wasn't a decision, it was a helpless act."

Before and during the book's creation, Harrison spent five years in analysis. Folks don't undertake that process to make up a pretty bedtime story starring themselves, but to find out what the hell happened. When Harrison announced the move to nonfiction to her husband, he said, "I feel like the chemo has begun." To finish the book, she did a slog of sixteen-hour days over six months. "In therapy, the window had come open, and I didn't know how long it could stay that way."

So many reviewers deemed her motives venal, but if you deduct the cost of mandatory therapy to get through the story in her heart before undertaking the book's writing, she'd have made more money working a deep-fat fryer, which might have also been more fun.

But with such personal reasons for writing, why publish it at all?

To understand, you'd have to marshal some empathy for any rape or incest survivor. It's through shame and silence that a perpetrator seeks to capture someone else's soul, sentencing her to lifetime collusion with him. "On top of everything else," Harrison told me, "I was supposed to keep my mouth shut forever." Either she published her story or remained complicit with her seducer, which meant actually being allied with him against herself. Publishing the book was a way to reclaim "what was left of me."

Harrison is a study in the courage a book can demand from its scribbler. From page one, you can hear her resolve to treat her young self—to my eye, anyway—to fairly unblinking scrutiny. The voice has the brutal detachment of a traumatized girl in a dissociative state during a rape. Or like some doomed prisoner speaking from inside an iron mask. Which—psychically speaking—seems apt.

> We meet at airports. We meet in cities we've never been to before. We meet where no one will recognize us.
> One of us flies, the other brings a car, and in it we set out for some destination. Increasingly, the places we go are unreal places: the Petrified Forest, Monument Valley, the Grand Canyon—places as stark and beautiful and deadly as those revealed in satellite photographs of distant planets. Airless, burning, inhuman.
> Against such backdrops, my father takes my face in his hands. He tips it up and kisses my closed eyes, my throat. I feel his fingers in the hair at the nape of my neck. I feel his hot breath on my eyelids.

We quarrel sometimes, and sometimes we weep.
The road always stretches endlessly ahead and behind
us, so that we are out of time as well as out of place.

She cuts herself no slack. It's *we* meet, *we* quarrel, *we* weep. She speaks as an adult choosing, not as a girl with a gun to her head.

Rather than praise the obvious precision and grace of this prose, *Vanity Fair*'s Michael Shnayerson calls Harrison "a tease" for not making herself smutty enough. It's a painful book but not a sexually explicit one—an almost impossible feat given the topic. (Actually, the most carnal scene in *The Kiss* paints Harrison's disinterested mother standing alongside a gynecologist's table as he deflowers the girl with increasing large penis substitutes so she can go off to college with a diaphragm, and not get pregnant at seventeen as Harrison's mother had with her.) Shnayerson's "Women Behaving Badly" rebukes those of us who had the temerity to write about sexual assault or other psychic travails at all.

The *Washington Post*'s Jonathan Yardley wrote three pieces lambasting Harrison: "It is a measure of the times that this book, slimy, repellent, meretricious, cynical, is enjoying the rapt attention of the gods of publicity." He accused her not only of fabrication ("Harrison claims") but of financial motives: "This confession isn't from the heart, it's from the pocketbook." In the *New Republic*, James Wolcott equated the book with reenacting Harrison's abuse on her three children. (In fact, Harrison and her husband chose to bring the book out while the kids were too young to twig to the media furor.) Shnayerson and Yardley and their fellows all used the same patronizing and pious tone critics once brought to scolding Charlotte Brontë for her novels' excessive emotion. *How dare she!*

It's hard for me to comprehend reading Harrison's story with zero feeling for the daughter, particularly one who doesn't sugarcoat her own role. Not only does the father cudgel a young woman desperate for his love into a sex act; he also claims she's his forever because he's polluted her: "Nobody will ever want to touch you after what I've done." (He actually hopes she'll bear his child so it'll be 75 percent him!) Who could wish silence on a woman who'd had such a run-in?

Harrison may have written to reclaim her own future, but by breaking the silence about incest, she no doubt rescued countless others. Rather than vilify her, critics should've given her a medal for public service.

19 | Old-School Technologies for the Stalled Novice

Yes, I felt very small. The typewriter seemed larger than a piano, I was less than a molecule. What could I do? I drank more.

Albert Sánchez Piñol, *Pandora in the Congo*

It's tough to keep going when you hit a roadblock in your own work. Many beginners just need to keep their heads in the game and their hands moving across pages till they gain traction. Some people tout writing exercises, but they never yielded squat to me. I'd encourage you to find intellectual enterprises to keep you studying craft. Maybe try some of the tools I've used to keep my ass in the chair, learning from my betters. Some of these involve writing longhand, shoving a gel-tip across an expanse. It will slow you down as typing can't.

1. Keep a commonplace book: a notebook where you copy beloved poems or hunks of prose out. Nothing will teach you a great writer's choices better. Plus

you can carry your inspiration around with you in compact form.

2. Write reviews or criticism for an online blog or a magazine—it'll discipline you to find evidence for your opinions and make you a crisper thinker.

3. Augment a daily journal with a reading journal. Compose a one-page review with quotes. Make yourself back up opinions. You can't just say, "Neruda is a surrealist"; you have to quote him watching laundry "from which slow dirty tears are falling." And you have to look up something about surrealism to define it.

4. Write out longhand on three-by-five-inch index cards quotes you come across—writer's name on the left, source and page on the right. (Stanley Kunitz taught me this circa 1978. I now have thousands of these, from which I cobble up lectures.)

5. Memorize poems when you're stuck. Poets teach you more about economy—not wasting a reader's time.

6. Write longhand letters to your complicated characters, or even to the dead. You'll learn more about voice by writing letters—how you arrange yourself different ways for each audience—than in a year of classes.

20 | Major Reversals in *Cherry* and *Lit*

The idea that the looker affects the sight is taken for granted in every field of scientific enquiry today, but one needs to be clear about what it does (and does not) mean. It does not mean "everything is subjective anyway," so that no clear and truthful statements can be made.

Robert Hughes, *The Shock of the New*

Warning label: For decades, lecture audiences have questioned me at length about the roller-coaster reversals of my second and third books, *Cherry* and *Lit*. I know nobody else's reversals intimately enough to set them down. Some of this I've glanced past in other writing, and while repeating myself is anathema, the lessons belong here. Whether you're a practitioner or not, if you can't suffer another word about my own work, feel free to bound over this to the next chapter.

With my second and third books, I overturned my comfy takes on the past as I'd never done in *Liars' Club* once I began it as nonfiction. In both later books, I kept bumbling into holes in my theories about my teen and early adult years, long-held ideas that had zero evidence in fact.

It started with *Cherry*'s first chapter as I tried to render saying a weepy good-bye to my old man before heading out to

California in a truck full of surfers and heads. All my life, I'd relied on the premise that Daddy had abandoned me a decade before I took off. So I was shopping for a scene to show the reader his abandonment and perhaps dab a tear from my living eye as I did so.

But I could find no scene to exemplify his abandonment. I'd be at work, and he'd bring me a supper plate wrapped in foil. He'd offer to make me breakfast in the morning or to take me squirrel hunting or fishing; I'd say no. I was the one who shrugged his hand off my shoulder. I was the one who kept quiet Mother's dalliances with a cowboy on a Colorado vacation. I was the one about to head for the California coast.

Of course, he drank like a fish, and his emotional stoicism made him the strong, silent type. And he ignored my mother's madness in ways that didn't protect us from her. But he never said he'd be somewhere for me and didn't show up, and he hated like hell when I left home.

That about-face took me by storm, though. I'd spent decades discussing his abandonment in therapy, and it was true he'd drunk himself off a barstool when I was just twenty-five. But the view that he'd ever left me was tacit hogwash—a convenient lie I'd told myself to salve my own guilt about leaving him.

The other bubble that got burst in *Cherry* was the long-held conviction that I'd been supersmart as a teenager—a real brainiac. But foraging around, I found zero evidence for this. I bailed out of advanced math after tenth grade. My grades sucked—I got a D in art. For every great book I read (*Anna Karenina*), I took in ten crap counterculture tomes (Eldridge Cleaver's *Soul on Ice* or Abbie Hoffman's *Steal This Book*).

If I wasn't smart, where on earth did I get this idea? Well, compared to the dope dealers I hung out and later roomed with—guys who did serious prison bids and who died young (knife fight, AIDS, gunshot to the temple, carbon dioxide in the garage)—I was a genius. Mostly, though, I was a fan of eggheads—my best girl pal was the smartest in school. She and two guys I dated seriously aced the big standardized tests and sifted through scholarship offers by the mailbox full. I only posed as a smart person.

But that reversal—rather than being something I'd hide— actually buffed up my material, because it exposed the schism between who I'd wanted to be and who I'd actually been. That's the stuff of inner conflict and plot.

The book had been a burr in my head for ten years. I wanted it to fill a hole I saw in the memoir canon. Not only did girls not write about sex in high school—other than assaults or aberrant sex—they hardly rendered adolescence at all. Many polevaulted from childhood to college.

Men's coming-of-age memoirs were jam-packed with adolescent rebellion, including early erotics—Frank McCourt kept "interfering" with himself and was seduced by an older woman in *Angela's Ashes*. The child Harry Crews boinks an older girl under a porch.

Watching a girl in the library behind bookshelves, Frank Conroy finds in a glimpse of breast that the world has become "suddenly harmonious." His poetic language eschews the pornographic but makes a masturbation scene first tender, then terrifying.

> With exquisite care I made the necessary adjustments
> and delved into myself. Hello old friend. Companion
> in the wilderness. Gift-giver.
>   I moved a few books and found her, or rather found
> a piece of her, neck to breast in white cotton. . . . In
> this state, one sees with the clarity of a mystic. A
> breast, a wrist, a curved hip become images of pure
> significance, passing directly into the tenderest part of
> the brain.

While he's in this state of intense focus, the view shifts and he suddenly sees that she's weeping in anguish: "I recoiled from the peephole as if a needle had pierced my pupil."

His scene in the chapter "Losing My Cherry" shows him transformed by the process.

> Her sex was no longer simply the entrance way
> one penetrated in search of deeper, more tangible
> mysteries. It had become, all at once, *slippery*—a
> lush blossom beyond which there was no need to
> go.
>   Afterward, I lay still, dazzled.

But there was no comparable passage I could find among the women memoirists I admired. They just skipped over desire— puberty and masturbation were swept past, and sex arrived at a decent age in clinical portrayals.

Except for the aberrant—Maya Angelou in *I Know Why the Caged Bird Sings* describes a childhood assault, complete with the guilt she felt about "the nice part": "He held me so softly that I wished he'd never let me go." But he's only warming up to raping her so violently:

> Then there was the pain. A breaking and entering
> when even the senses are torn apart. The act of rape
> on an eight-year-old body is a matter of the needle
> giving because the camel can't. The child gives,
> because the body can and the mind of the violator
> cannot. I thought I had died.

Her sense of culpability mirrored my own, and my conviction that she was innocent helped me start to think I might be
too. "Mr. Freeman had surely done something very wrong, but
I was convinced that I had helped him to do it." (When the
rapist was freed early and found kicked to death behind the
slaughterhouse, I felt a sick sense of justice.)

Yet when Angelou's in college and sleeps with a boy, there's
zero description. Kathryn Harrison's college beau is likewise
never described in any intimate way—nor her sexual reac-
tions.

Mary McCarthy's *Memories of a Catholic Girlhood* comes
closest to the subject, but she has more erotic feelings when she
buys a book: "I was tremendously excited by this act. It was the
first expensive book I had ever bought with my own money."
Compare this to her impressions of the married man she drinks
and makes out with in a hotel.

> I grew a little tired of his kisses, which did not excite
> me, perhaps because they were always the same. . . . I
> was only precocious mentally and lived in deadly fear
> of losing my virtue, not for moral reasons, but from
> the dread of being thought "easy."

Later, when in *How I Grew* she loses her virginity, she's also completely without desire as she makes out with her guy in a parked car:

> I was wildly excited but not sexually excited. At
> the time, though, I was unaware of there being
> a difference between mental arousal and specific
> arousal of the genital organs. This led to many
> misunderstandings. . . .
>
> In fact, he became very educational, encouraging
> me to sit up and examine his stiffened organ,
> which to me looked quite repellent, all flushed and
> purplish. . . .
>
> Of the actual penetration, I remember nothing. It
> was as if I had been given chloroform.

This writing is physically removed and clinical—"genital organs" and "penetration." I presume it was the age she dwelt in, but I couldn't find any clues to her having a body at all. It was like the film they showed us on such things in health class circa 1960.

Embarking on *Cherry*, I was prepared to overhaul all the tepid writing about puberty that women from the more prudent past had used to glaze over desire.

But the minute I hit the page, I saw the problem. Male adolescence is mondo celebrated in our culture—all of rock and roll exists to cheer on guys grabbing their crotches and humping mikes as preamble to reproducing the species. And men have all these great childish words—*chubbie* and *woodie*—that permit them to sound full of desire yet oddly innocent. There's no comparable language for girls. Applied to a prepubescent girl, the standard nomenclature just sounds violently wrong. The writing I was doing to represent my early feelings actually made me feel like some Lolita luring pedophiles.

Finally, it came to me: as I'd been working, I'd unconsciously superimposed my thirty-something libido onto my child self. The feelings felt "untrue" because they were. What I'd been leaving out was the hazy, soft-focus obsession with being loved that really preoccupied my girl self—all the sappy romantic notions that formed the basis of my early fantasies were completely G-rated. Being boy-crazy was not being sex-crazy. I didn't fantasize being boffed into guacamole. Rather, I imagined the boy I liked at the roller rink skating over to me during the couples skate with one red rose.

How unsexy that was—uncool in every way. Yet that became my challenge, to create the trance state that comes of writing a boy's name on your notebook ten times or watching him on the football field, imagining he'll run over to give you a hug.

I wound up trying to capture early-teen desire in the poetic, metaphorical way it had come to me then. There's nothing porno about it, and yet it carries massive intensity. Also, I'd chosen *Cherry* as an ironic title: I felt—due to household upheaval and two childhood rapes—I'd lost my innocence long before I should have. But the more I wrote, the more I discovered that innocence had never left me, if you measure innocence as a capacity for belief—particularly a belief in love. What was mine in terms of hope and sweet longing had been with me all along—still, in some ways, is.

In *Lit*, I was also bedeviled by letting present knowledge block out clear memories of the past. I just couldn't stop seeing my marriage except colored by our divorce, and I wrote the same pages over and over, not making stuff up, but canting the material one way, then another. At first I wrote events that cast him as perfect and me as a drunken slag. Then I wrote him as an icy WASP and myself as a tender heart. None of it rang emotionally true to me. I despaired. I even considered giving back the advance, which I'd have had to sell my apartment to do.

Then after meditation one day, when I'd prayed for the seventh month running for some glimpse of the truth, I had a vivid flash of us young and in love, floating in inner tubes down a Vermont river the week we met. How tender we'd been. The memory brought a stab of pain almost physical—I'd avoided writing about how in love we were, brimming with hope. It had been far easier to make glib, jokey remarks about how shitty a wife I'd been.

Dumb hope is what it hurts most to write, occupying the foolish schemes we pursued for decades, the blind alleys, the cliffs we stepped off. If you find yourself blocked for a period, maybe goad yourself in the direction of how you hoped at the time. Ask yourself if you aren't strapping your current self across the past to hide the real story.

21 | Why Memoirs Fail

My last memory is the Headmaster's parting shot:
"Well, good-bye, Graves, and remember that your best
friend is the waste-paper basket." This has proved good
advice . . . . few writers seem to send their work through
as many drafts as I do.

Robert Graves, *Good-Bye to All That*

Most memoirs fail because of voice. It's not distinct enough to sound alive and compelling. Or there are staunch limits to emotional tone, so it emits a single register. Being too cool or too shrill can ruin the read. The sentences are boring and predictable, or it's so inconsistent you don't know who's speaking or what place they come from. You don't believe or trust the voice. You're not curious about the inner or outer lives of the writer. The author's dead in the water.

We live in the age of the image, and it's too easy to learn carnal writing for a memoirist to sketch a foggy physical world sans evocative sensory detail. A lot of instruction manuals beam in on the physical, simply because you *can* master it. But few textbooks take up how the inner life manifests itself in a memoir's pages. In the more spectacular visual media like action films, say, the inner life fails to get much airplay—at most a scene in a shrink's office or a snippet of voiceover here and there. But memoir can compete against the pyrotechnics of visual imagery in film and TV only by excelling where those media fail: writing a deeper moment from *inside* it.

You're looking for that inner enemy that'll help you to structure the book. I always have inklings of it, but tend to find it by writing interior frets and confessions and yearnings as I recall them. Maybe it's only manifest after a first draft. Once I've found it, I'll revise with it as the spine—how the self evolves to reconcile its inner conflicts over time. Your attendant setbacks and jackpots should lead up to a transformed self at the end.

Another way a crap memoir fails is if the narrator fails to change over time. Characters who don't transform or who lack depth become predictable. If the bad characters were consistently bad in real life, it would make all our heartbreaks almost palatable. We could just steer clear of the always-hateful human. But the hateful are kind sometimes, or sorry—or they *sound* so sincerely sorry it's hard not to get lured in again and again. Those of us who grew up with seductive narcissists in the family know that they capture you not with their bullying but by somehow making you pity them in private. So you imagine you're the sole confidante of this individual's inner misery. She needs your fealty, and you give it repeatedly despite brutal evidence that doing so puts you in danger.

Shallow reportage usually stems from a lack of psychological self-knowledge. The narrator is always tough or stoical or self-sacrificing, or always ready with the quick quip or smart-ass posture. Worst of all, such characters are hackneyed as hell, predictable when life often fails to be and art must never be.

Most stale of all is the butt-whipping memoir, which abounds these days: "I took a butt-whipping, I got up and took another. Poor me, here came yet another." The great Holocaust memoirs portray not just great suffering but great hope and wisdom and forms of psychological endurance and curiosity. They seem written to help us understand something complex, not to prove a single point in dreary repetition. A book that concerns itself only with one thing—*I Was a Teenage Sex Slave*, say—might have some prurient interest, but unless that thing is super dramatic (a war or a concentration camp) or varied in its portrayal, you won't find yourself rereading it.

Unless there's a political motive (as for Robert Graves or Richard Wright), a bitter book grows tired, a vengeful one unreadable. You know the writer's morphing every event to make a point.

Or a memoir fails from a pacing problem—it goes fast over dramatic events and slows to a snail's pace to dispense banal information or go on a tangent.

You can be too smotheringly close to an event, so it's over-powering to the reader. Or you keep your distance, so just when something key is about to be revealed, it becomes glib or jokey.

I remember a piece in which a closeted gay writer was about to get laid for the first time after pages of shame and fear. He goes to the disco, gets picked up, makes out at the bar, then—finally—brings the guy home. At the denouement, the author pole-vaults entirely out of the scene to launch into a long disquisition on his PhD dissertation, which ended the whole piece. Certainly you can pull the shade on a physical scene for discretion's sake. You don't have to detail a sex act as porn does. But the psychic swerve—not describing how the act affected the speaker—denied the reader what the writer had been promising for pages.

On the most basic level, bad sentences make bad books. Poet Robert Hass taught me you can rewrite a poem by making every single line better. I revise and revise and revise. Any editor of mine will tell you how crappy my early drafts are. Revisions are about clarifying and evoking feelings in the reader in the same way they were once evoked in me. Or how I see them now.

In *Lit*, my rough draft of one chapter started thus:

> Mother drove me to college in our yellow station wagon, and every night we stayed at a Holiday Inn, where we got drunk on screwdrivers.

This is information. Getting drunk with your mother suggests an emotional problem, but there's no inherent drama or conflict. Other than the yellow car, there's no carnality. The screwdrivers suggest trouble but don't really capture the emotional tenor of the drive. Mostly, there is no scene—just reportage of data. That's all I started with.

So how did I get from Draft 1's dried-up little sound bite to something lusher? Memory—a physical memory of that time, a carnal fact. The car hadn't come with air conditioning, so Mother installed a cheap one, which hung from the dash. It collected distillation, so when she made a sharp right turn, icy water—faintly redolent of chemical coolant—would slosh out onto my bare feet. Getting doused by that splash of freezing condensation was like a physical baptism miraculously dousing me in that single, living instant. It's as if memory's eye suddenly flipped open.

Like many such scenes, it comes to me in florid present tense. I look down and see the giant bamboo-bottom flip-flops I'd bought in California, with their black velvet straps, getting drenched with cold water. And I am in that car again. I can see the derby hat Mother wore—a pimp hat, she called it. She'd bought me one, too, in Houston. And she wears a copper bracelet that turns her wrist green because somebody told her it helps with arthritis in her hand. And another sense memory comes: I smell peaches, which we bought by the bushel in Arkansas. Also vodka from the screwdrivers Mother drank all the way down.

I rest inside those sense memories, and a phrase comes to me—peaches galore. Mother says we have peaches galore, and I say, Wasn't that some burlesque dancer's name? And Mother says, That was Pussy Galore. Her saying the word *pussy* is almost as wince-inducing as watching the savagery with which she devours a peach. And I remember feeling cooped up with her—a luxury in some ways, since her attention was hard to come by. But I also recall longing to run away. Those conflicting desires held the emotional fuel in that chapter.

And the memories start flying at me like bats swooping out of the past—my reading aloud to her an early English version of *One Hundred Years of Solitude*. That novel makes it in, and the phrase about Pussy Galore; the derby hats do a cameo. But the copper bracelet and the air conditioner vanish. And that beautiful Iowa corn, the sheer order and wealth of it—those rich farms with large white houses—that's the kind of American scene I longed to enter. It opposes my squalid hometown and Mother's own Dust Bowl childhood.

The cornfield is an apt symbol for what I aspired to, at the time. Folks from normal childhoods might fear the tidy repetition of the rows. To me, they looked like an order that lent comfort. So I used the image to begin the chapter.

> Mother's yellow station wagon slid like a Monopoly
> icon along the gray road that cut between fields
> of Iowa corn, which was chlorophyll green and
> punctuated in the distance by gargantuan silver silos
> and gleaming, unrusted tractors glazed cinnamon
> red. Mother told me how the wealth of these farmers
> differed from the West Texas dirt farmers of her Dust
> Bowl youth, who doled out mortgaged seed from
> croaker sacks.
>
> But because I was seventeen and had bitten my
> cuticles raw facing the prospect of fitting in at the
> private college we'd reach that night—which had
> accepted me through some mixture of pity and
> oversight—and because I was split-headed with the
> hangover Mother and I had incurred the night before
> sucking down screwdrivers in the unaptly named
> Holiday Inn in Kansas City, I told Mother something
> like, Enough already about your shitty youth. You've
> told me about eight million times since we pulled out
> of the garage.

It has a carnal description—the car like a Monopoly icon—from a point of view I could only have in imagination. Other carnal facts: the girl me has both a hangover and bitten cuticles. In addition to data from the earlier draft that this mother-daughter team get drunk together at night, it gives background info that the first paragraph lacks:

- Mother's Dust Bowl youth
- The author's age
- Where she's from

- That she's a worrier
- That the college she's heading to is one above her station
- The blight of her shitty high school record

So there exists a boatload of interior information that helps to create emotional conflicts:

- The mother's low-rent background adds to the daughter's angst about going to a fancier college than normal in that family.
- The daughter telling the mother she's sick of hearing about said mother's shitty youth shows the somewhat normal conflict between mother and daughter, though for a daughter to call her mother's youth "shitty" was way outside the mores of that time. The idiom suggests a lack of boundary between the two that gestures to the book's central conflict.

In addition, I explain several things about my notion of truth:

- The Monopoly icon image says I am using imagined scenes from my adult point of view.
- Saying "I told Mother something like" proves I'm reconcocting talk, not working from a diary or objective script.

Most of all, the scene holds core emotional truths that will eventually shape the whole book. The teen me wanted to be like Mother—artistic, boho. We wind up reading a great novel together. But wanting to become Mother doomed me to become a drunk, an emotional car wreck, and not much of a nurturer. I mean, she got potted nightly with seventeen-year-old me as if we were sorority sisters. Teen me also longed to escape my suckhole hometown, which Mother likewise resented and blamed me for keeping her stranded in—so to add to my angst, I felt guilty leaving her behind. The revision tries to infuse the scene with some undercurrent of the psychic torrents trapped in that car's small space—two squirrels in a coffee can, Daddy might have said.

22 | An Incomplete Checklist to Stave Off Dread

Plain words on plain paper. Remember what Orwell says, that good prose is like a windowpane. Cut every page you write by at least a third. Stop constructing those piffling little similes of yours. Work out what you want to say. Then say it in the most direct and vigorous way you can. Eat meat. Drink blood. Give up your social life and don't think you can have friends. Rise in the quiet hours of the night and prick your fingertips and use the blood for ink; that will cure you of persiflage!

But do I take my own advice? Not a bit. Persiflage is my nom de guerre. (Don't use foreign expressions. It's elitist.)

Hilary Mantel, *Giving Up the Ghost*

For those of you with a naturally generative talent, able to bang out pages by the ream, this chapter may only help you later in the process, when it's time to revise and organize and tighten. But mostly I'm writing for that human creature who sits down brimming with a story, then thinks, Oh, shit. What first?

This chapter answers that, so far as I can. It should also lend some comfort: ts'ok to be lost. Being lost—as I've said else-where—is a prelude to finding new paths. And any curious writer will have to do a lot of wandering before any book's done. You won't have most of your elements on day one. You should have:

1. Crisp memories—that carnal world in your head
2. Stories and a passion to tell them
3. Some introductory information or data to get across
4. The self-discipline to work in scary blankness for some period of time (for me it takes three to five weeks to find a way in, though I've been in the weeds for a year at a pop)

Everything else, you can figure out as you go. In fact, if you start telling your stories, the pieces tend to fall into place. As you work, you're looking for those other elements mentioned before—a voice that exploits your talent and an interior point of view, complete with an inner enemy to organize the book around.

Writers hate formulas and checklists. It's way more fun to masquerade as a natural shaman who channels beautiful pages as the oracle once channeled Zeus. But looking at my own books, I've found they all include most of the stuff below—as do most of the books I teach.

Here's my list:

1. Paint a physical reality that uses all the senses and exists in the time you're writing about—a singular, fascinating place peopled with objects and characters we believe in. Should include the speaker's body or some kinesthetic elements.
2. Tell a story that gives the reader some idea of your milieu and exploits your talent. We remember in stories, and for a writer, story is where you start.
3. Package information about your present self or backstory so it has emotional conflict or scene.

All the rest of these are interior:

4. Set emotional stakes—why is the writer passionate about or desperate to deal with the past—the hint of an inner enemy?

5. Think, figure, wonder, guess. Show yourself weighing what's true, your fantasies, values, schemes, and failures.

6. Change times back and forth—early on, establish the "looking back" voice, and the "being in it" voice.

7. Collude with the reader about your relationship with the truth and memory.

8. Show not so much how you suffer in long passages, but how you survive. Use humor or an interjecting adult voice to help a reader over the dark places.

9. Don't exaggerate. Trust that what you felt deeply is valid.

10. Watch your blind spots—in revision, if not before, search for reversals. Beware of what you avoid and what you cling to.

11. (Related to all of the above) Love your characters. Ask yourself what underlay their acts and versions of the past. Sometimes I pray to see people I'm angry at or resentful or as God sees them, which heals both page and heart.

And one big fat caveat: lead with your own talent, which may cause you to ignore all I've recommended.

23 | Michael Herr: Start in Kansas, End in Oz

Oh, return to zero, the master said.
Use what's lying around the house.
Make it simple and sad.

Stephen Dunn, "Visiting the Master"

I. What He Does

Every reader who didn't fall for Michael Herr's voice in his seminal war memoir *Dispatches* (1977) fell for it as a moviegoer in the haunting narration of *Apocalypse Now* or his later script for Stanley Kubrick's *Full Metal Jacket*, both of which echo the book:

> How many people had I already killed? There was those six that I know about for sure. Close enough to blow their last breath in my face. But this time it was an American and an officer. That wasn't supposed to make any difference to me, but it did. Shit . . . charging a man with murder in this place was like handing out speeding tickets in the Indy 500. I took the mission. What the hell else was I gonna do? But I didn't know what I'd do when I found him.
>
> Charley didn't get much USO. He was dug in too

deep or moving too fast. His idea of great R&R was
cold rice and a little rat meat. He had only two ways
home: death, or victory.

Apocalypse Now

Michael Herr invented what Americans think of as the
hypnotic, surreal sounds of that awful war (maybe any awful
war), and it made him famous in a movie genre I've heard him
darkly refer to as Vietnam porn.

Dispatches landed the unassuming Syracuse dropout in the
upper echelon of literati working in English. (John le Carré
called it "the best book I have ever read on men and war in our
time.") The Vietnam War era perhaps ushered in the great age
of the liar—Nixon confessing that he'd been bombing Cambodia all along after denying it, his collusions with Watergate
burglars, his paranoid tapes.

In the 1970s, kids like me who found Herr's work in *Rolling
Stone* or *Esquire* cherished him as the folk hero who'd called
bullshit on the government reports we'd been fed about Vietnam for decades. Enemy body counts had been beefed up, a
fact later confirmed in defense secretary Robert S. McNamara's
memoir. Our massive bombing runs had so decimated and ex-
foliated the country that we could never win the people's faith.
("We never announced a scorched-earth policy, we never announced any policy.") Drugs we went to jail for in the States
were practically handed out with mess kits over there, and
My Lai wasn't an isolated incident. Herr's cynicism about the
big dogs made him a beacon. He even dubbed high command
"The Mission"—ironically marrying military goals with so-
called spiritual ones. In Vietnam, Herr tells us, whether we

came feigning or intending rescue or not, we still wound up invaders.

So Herr's über-trippy view actually came off as "truer" than the other war noises we'd heard; but his was that new truth—it came with quotes around it. I sometimes wonder if *Dispatches* doesn't mark that place in history when subjective truth began its rise to supplant historical and religious certainties—a trend that helped the current craze for memoir along. Coincidence doesn't imply causality, but still. However a warped memory might have marred Herr's unique take on that bloody patch of history, we trusted him more than we did officialdom, perhaps because he wrote like he was on acid half the time. He lacked the steely piety of official government dispatches. And his passionate sense of his own moral culpability—even for just watching the war—affirmed our national feelings of shame about the conflict.

Herr claims much of *Dispatches* is mashed-up characters and unchecked facts. (It was published as fiction in France.) Despite that, he recently told me he cared about nothing so much as veracity. He'd gone half nuts trying to write it, his wife coming home to find him in a chair surrounded by wadded up yellow legal-pad pages, and then, "I finally gave myself a kind of permission that I'd been reluctant to give to write about certain things. Now it sounds so pompous to say it—a truth telling."

While other reporters went out with troops for short stints, then came in to wire stories on deadline, Herr had no deadlines. He'd stay embedded for months, and all that time, he was cramming his notebook, capturing dialogue that still prowls my head—" 'We had this gook, and we was gonna skin him' (a

grunt told me). 'I mean he was already dead and everything.' "
Herr's talent rests in weaving together conflicting voices, jux-
taposing dialogue from all over, the tender and the monstrous
side by side. He speaks in rock-and-roll lyrics, hippie aphorisms,
hep-cat ebonics, army acronyms, and the pop religion of redneck grunts, and lacing it all together is his own elegiac longing for some solid ground he never really finds.

This talent for capturing unforgettable dialogue no doubt
grew from a childhood of innocent curiosity about strangers. Playing detective as a kid, he mastered memorizing the
spoken word at an age when his peers were fixated on their
Little League swings: "I was a voyeur. . . . I trained myself to
eavesdrop while looking out the train window and not to miss
a word. I used to walk around when I was twelve and follow
people home. This would involve even taking bus rides with
them. I just wanted to see where and how they lived" (*Los An-
geles Times*, April 15, 1990). The fractured poetry of American
idiom naturally enthralled him, and he cultivated an ear for the
small majesty of the average human unit speaking.

Herr confesses that much of *Dispatches* was pieced together.
But he stands by the quotes that ring so true: "Very few lines
were literally invented." In other words, the voices that trans-
fix us—and for me form the core of his talent—may be the
closest to verbatim reportage.

Plus his lack of historical method is moot anyway. We read
Herr not to nail down external events—the date of this bombing raid or that regimental movement—but to share the journey of the narrator's terrified, puzzled, heartbroken, outraged
psyche. The landscape he reports on never stops shape-shifting.
So blurry and hallucinatory is his crazy-quilt collage, you'd no
more look to him for facts than a court would privilege an eye-

witness on 'shrooms at the time. Listen to how he appropriates the bureaucratic natter about why we were there—and ends with a scary truth about why *he* was:

> [You'd] hear some overripe bullshit about it: Hearts and minds, Peoples of the Republic, tumbling dominoes, maintaining the equilibrium of the Dingdong by containing the ever encroaching Doodah. "All that's just a *load*, man. We're here to kill gooks. Period." Which wasn't at all true of me. I was there to watch.

We emerge from his sentence about Dingdong and Doodah into the presence of a young grunt hungry for murder, and from that into Herr's dark vigilance—*I was there to watch*—which comes with a backwash of being mortified. "You want to look and you don't want to look."

This moral struggle shapes that inner enemy I keep squawking about. Like Hemingway before him, Herr had gone to war in part to satisfy his young man's thirst for adventure—an obscene wish, he later felt. His desire to be there implicated him, as if Vietnam were a giant snuff film he supported by buying a ticket to it. Seeing the dead was like looking at "all the porn in the world."

> I could've looked till my lamps went out and still wouldn't have accepted the connection between a detached leg and the rest of the body or the poses and positions that always happened . . . making them lie anywhere and any way it left them, hanging over barbed wire or thrown promiscuously on top of other dead or up in the trees like terminal acrobats. *Look what I can do.*

He undercuts the drama of the scene with that black humor common among some vets—the dead like acrobats, saying, *Look what I can do.*

The moral certainty he craves always eludes him, for lies and mystery cover every scene. *Spooky* is a word he uses, a phrase coming from a pop song of the day. A soldier enigmatically says, "Spooky understands." And Herr's able to make us feel both the vastness of that mystery and the chilling breath of wind around some ghosts that haunt him. He doesn't obscure facts or withhold them—he says everything he can about what he's staring at, and it still denies him any certainty. He makes it sound as if many people survive war by grasping a single truth—*Those people were monsters we had to destroy*, say—clutching it like a god, while a thousand conflicting truths go unstudied.

Herr never makes himself a figure of pity, but I disagree with a reviewer who claimed the book is not about him. It's not in the sense that he's never doing what Leo Tolstoy blames Ivan Turgenev for—"pointing to the tear in his eye." As with many great memoirists, you are never not behind his eyes.

The carnage, of course, sparks a natural urge toward moral outrage, a position that demands somebody be blamed. But blame makes deep compassion impossible, and in spiritual terms—which is what Herr grows into by book's end, when he becomes a Buddhist—only compassion can bring about deep healing. He can never reconcile the beauty and joy he found in the war with the horror—"It wreaks havoc on the Western mind," he notes. "It was way off the ordinary scale of good and bad. It's just another level." For Herr, the war's gorgeous polyglot of voices—however beautiful and horrifying and, in his word, *glamorous*—keeps the nature of information fluid. The constantly mutating landscape prevents him from finding a moral stance that doesn't include rage at somebody—rage, again, serving as a compassion blocker. Nowhere is ethical judgment more desperately called for, and nowhere is it more impossible.

His tenderness for the young soldiers is infectious. "I had such love for them and thought I wasn't supposed to," he says. They were capable of profound barbarity: "[They] threw people out of helicopters, tied people up and put the dogs on them." But those same young men also took bullets for each other and threw themselves on grenades. They quite literally kept him alive, laying down fire for him in a hot zone so he could dash to a helicopter whenever he fled a place they were often doomed to die in. They offered to hump Herr's pack or give him the only warm sleeping spot in a wet trench (he never let them). Herr admires, pities, adores, and shrinks from them over the course of the book: "I stood as close to them as I could without actually being one of them, and then I stood as far back as I could without leaving the planet."

Herr's compassion for the soldiers—"How do you feel when a nineteen-year-old kid tells you from the bottom of his heart that he's gotten too old for this shit?"—somehow mitigates his horror, and ours:

> Was it possible they were there and not haunted? No, not possible, not a chance, I know I wasn't the only one. Where are they now? (Where am I now?). . . . But disgust was only one color in the whole mandala, gentleness and pity were other colors. . . . I think all those people who used to say they only wept for the

Vietnamese never really wept for anyone at all if they couldn't squeeze out at least one for those men and boys when they died or had their lives cracked open for them.

But of course we were intimate, I'll tell you how intimate: they were my guns, and I let them do it. We covered each other, an exchange of services. . . .

Talk about impersonating an identity, about locking into a role, about irony: I went to cover the war and the war covered me. . . . I went there behind the crude but serious belief that you had to be able to look at anything, serious because I acted on it and went, crude because I didn't always know what you were seeing until later, maybe years later, that a lot of it never made it in at all, it just stayed there in your eyes. Time and information, rock and roll, life itself, the information isn't frozen, you are.

The book's darkness relents in the clown play of the Mission. I spit coffee reading his interview with General William Westmoreland. Sending Herr in to speak with him is like sending the visionary William Blake into the tent of Attila the Hun. The general expects, since Herr's from *Esquire*, that he's "writing 'humoristical' pieces."

I came away feeling as though I'd just had a conversation with a man who touches a chair and says "This is a chair," points to a desk and says, "This is a desk." I couldn't think of anything to ask him.

Herr's ability to mock "official military speak" rivals comic genius Joseph Heller in *Catch-22*. Herr will set out by quoting somebody, and then he'll twist out of present reality, reeling the point of view inside his own head, where we "hear" through the warp of his psyche.

His interior is the home place for the reader, the helicopter pickup point. Whenever we wander off into some awful jungle scene, we do so alongside that richly observant speaker. It's Herr's desire for a solidity *inside*—for some truth—and his inability to get a firm grasp on that truth that keeps him fumbling around like a blind man.

Now a practicing Buddhist in a fairly rigorous (as I understand it) Tibetan mode, Herr recently told me by phone that before Vietnam he hadn't known we're not just responsible for all we do, but for all we see, too. This frees us from blaming or judging anybody. (In this, it echoes my Catholic notion of original sin—we're all the same!) "Great bodhisattvas get sick and die from taking on the suffering of others. They pray to be reborn in hell." (Hell being the first place Jesus went after the cross.)

Reading Michael Herr puts you in touch not just with the brutality we humans are capable of, but with some nobility that persists and persists and is made glorious by refusing defeat in horror's presence. It's not sweet and noble to die for one's country, but anyone who insists on leaning into the light in the face of so much darkness enacts perhaps the hardest-won of fortitudes.

A friend of mine recently diagnosed with one of the scarier cancers spoke of the unexpected comfort reading *Dispatches* gave him. On the phone, Herr was so touched. "Doesn't get any better than that. I always tell people, 'Don't worry, it has a happy ending.' "

II. How He Does It

(Note: Again, the lapidary work here—intended for the practitioner—may bore the general reader.)

If you bring a jeweler's loupe to Michael Herr's first chapter, analyzing it line by line the way poets do with a gloss or exegesis of an otherwise mysterious work, you can isolate that memoir's key machinery. That's what I get my grad students to do for any stylistic master—to pick apart one sentence at a time how a book's opener sets the terms for a whole book.

Read that way, Herr summarizes all of memoir's key elements. He lures us in with direct carnality, with information packaged in sizzling and evocative ways. His inner conflict never fades from you—the psychological stakes and that inner enemy that make the book cohere and lend us the impetus to keep reading stay on display. Mainly, he creates an intimate psychic space—a mind perceiving and remembering and analyzing and pondering with such variety that we cleave to it. Herr becomes, as you read him, as familiar and comforting as any friend.

A book known for its bizarre, hallucinatory surface opens with the cheapest writing of all—dull recorded fact, describing a static physical artifact. After coming back from the bush, Herr studies the antique map left on the wall. It's a quiet scene any reader can imagine herself inside. Then, line by line, he builds up to the jazzy surface his book is known for.

The map embodies the book's central worry—how "hard data" or "official information"—the stuff most reporters are shopping for—avoids the real impenetrable mystery of human suffering and nobility always evident in war's carnage. A "real" reporter trucks in simple data. Luckily for us, Herr clung to his talent—that poetic sensibility and ear for dialogue and story and atmosphere. He left hard facts to the trusted journalists, letting his true nature shine through.

> There was a map of Vietnam on the wall of my apartment
> in Saigon and some nights, I'd lie on my bed and look at
> it, too tired to do anything more than just get my boots
> off. That map was a marvel, especially now that it wasn't
> real anymore. For one thing, it was very old. It had
> been left there years before by another tenant, probably
> a Frenchman, since the map had been made in Paris.
> The paper had buckled in its frame after years in the wet
> Saigon heat, laying a kind of veil over the countries it
> depicted. Vietnam was divided into its older territories of
> Tonkin, Annam and Cochin China, and to the west past
> Laos and Cambodia sat Siam, a kingdom. That's old, I'd
> tell visitors, that's a really old map.
>   If dead ground could come back to haunt you the
> way dead people do, they'd have been able to mark my
> map CURRENT and burn the ones they'd been using
> since '64, but count on it, nothing like that was going to
> happen. It was late '67 now, even the most detailed
> maps didn't reveal much anymore; reading them was like
> trying to read the faces of the Vietnamese, and that was
> like trying to read the wind. We knew that the uses of
> most information were flexible, different pieces of
> ground told different stories to different people. We also
> knew that for years now there had been no country but
> the war.

1. Take it a phrase at a time. *There was a map of Vietnam.* If the current craze for over-the-top drama had affected the writing of *Dispatches*, Herr might have started with some fiery, guts-spilled war scene. Instead, he starts with a carnal object, and his reflection on it. A "true" thing—maps are meant to convey veracity. We should be able to find our way with them. He

starts in a small, almost dull, everyday object that just happens to be left behind in his transient's apartment.

2. *too tired to do anything more than just get my boots off.* Herr doesn't just tell us he's tired; he gives us dramatic evidence of the extent. It's another carnal moment of a type we all understand.

3. *That map was a marvel, especially now that it wasn't real anymore.* This is his interior interpretation of the map—it's a *marvel,* some kind of miraculous phenomenon, which is a theme that occupies most of the book. The phrase introduces his notion of unreality or impermeable mystery of war.

4. *For one thing, it was very old. It had been left there years before by another tenant, probably a Frenchman, since the map had been made in Paris.* Its antiqueness gives the map a kind of special radiance—a spiritual value, if you will. We also see Herr's mind feeling for the truth, guessing that since it was made in Paris, a Frenchman had probably left it. It's his first use of the word *probably*—the qualifier of a more truthful memoirist. He's showing us his mind in action, his thoughtfulness, and how he tries to deduce the truth based on hard evidence.

5. *The paper had buckled in its frame after years in the wet Saigon heat, laying a kind of veil over the countries it depicted.* This again is carnal evidence, conjuring the tropical feel of Saigon, a place whose soppy atmosphere insidiously seeps in to warp the map, as the war he'll show us will warp him and those he meets. The physical veil or mist acts as a physical metaphor, embodying the notion of "spookiness" or mystery. Whatever truth exists about the war is "veiled," as the map is.

6. *Vietnam was divided into its older territories of Tonkin, Annam and Cochin China, and to the west past Laos and Cambodia sat Siam, a kingdom.* These old places have an exotic echo, and Herr's listing them again shows his interest in historical information. Siam's being a kingdom brings up for my generation the musical *The King and I*. But even if you don't have those associations, its being a kingdom suggests an enchanted realm.

7. *If dead ground could come back to haunt you the way dead people do, they'd have been able to mark my map CURRENT and burn the ones they'd been using since '64.* Being haunted by the dead is a psychological driver for the book, and here's the first time Herr suggests burning up some dishonest depiction of the country—in this case the maps the military had been using. The disinformation of high command is part of what will obscure the truth for Herr—and, through him, for us—throughout the book. He calls them "they" here, making them separate from him, other. The capitalized CURRENT mimics an official stamp of the type military personnel used. The capitals suggest certainty, which—in Herr's view of this war—is always bogus. He occupies a visionary's demimonde.

8. *but count on it, nothing like that was going to happen.* The "count on it" is a little piece of hippie-esque locution that brings you inside the more intimate, colloquial speech Herr will use. The interjection forms a kind of bond with the reader. On a literal level, he's also saying the military will never rethink their maps' accuracy, because they lack the curiosity of fluidity of thought that makes changing their minds possible—and also makes truth impossible for them.

9. *It was late '67 now.* A simple statement of fact, this locates us in the time of his being there, at the height of the conflict. The phrase is also an infusion of quotidian reality after the "spookiness" of the sentence before.

10. *even the most detailed maps didn't reveal much anymore.* Again, you can't get true information from military maps and "official" evidence. We'll come to depend on the suggestively "spooky."

11. *reading them was like trying to read the faces of the Vietnamese, and that was like trying to read the wind.* This beautiful metaphor makes even the native citizens impossible to "read" or serve as a source, and it makes mysteries of the indigenous. The wind is also invisible, mysterious as the veil of moisture over the map or the ghosts that haunt him.

12. *We knew that the uses of most information were flexible, different pieces of ground told different stories to different people.* This is the first time Herr uses "we." It seems to mean everybody but high command, but in some ways it also invites the reader into his wondering. Again, the impossibility of locating the true "story" is what he wants throughout the book—what drives him.

13. *We also knew that for years now there had been no country but the war.* Despite all the disinformation, there is one fact "we"— him and other correspondents? him and everybody in the war? him and us readers?—know. I sort of think he encompasses all those possibilities. The war has devoured everything. The war *is* everything.

This setup about the curious uses of information leads us to Herr's first three characters. These three voices are the three main arenas of (dis)information—an American press official, who's clueless; a great, scary, medicated warrior in a tiger suit, a man at home in combat; and Herr himself as hypervigilant mediator, crouching in terror in combat. The press officer and the warrior are both confident in their beliefs; Herr's the confused one. And his confusion becomes our home, our certainty, our resting place.

The characters throw each other into relief, starting with the officer reporting in official speak. On a helicopter tour, he shows Herr from the air how strikes had leveled the ground beneath what had been the Ho Bo Woods—a place wholly denatured by chemicals and plows and endless fires, "wasting hundreds of acres of cultivated plantation and wild forest alike." Describing the process seems to thrill the officer, who's been telling the same story over and over to every visitor from "half the armies in the world." Herr's cool eye studies the guy's seeming thrill, letting him celebrate the story, till Herr eventually incorporates the guy's own voice into his interior. Herr's head just eats the guy's voice at the end, entering into a long sentence of official-sounding bullshit that warps at the end to Herr's judgment:

> It seemed to be keeping him young, his enthusiasm
> made you feel that even the letters he wrote home
> to his wife were full of it, it really showed what you
> could do if you had the knowhow and the hardware.
> . . . And if in the months following that operation
> incidences of enemy activity in the larger area of War
> Zone C had increased "significantly," and American
> losses had doubled and then doubled again, none of

it was happening in any damn Ho Bo Woods, you'd
better believe it.

This is the first time Herr appropriates somebody's voice to
channel it like a medium—"none of it was happening in any
damn Ho Bo Woods, you'd better believe it." Moving someone
else's voice into his own head is one way he makes you feel
intimate with him as a narrator and with the otherwise wild
experiences he writes about.

The officer's voice stands in stark contrast to the surreal
magic of Herr—a man "not nervously organized for war." He's
the next character, and we see him embedded with troops in
a state of profound, ass-clenching fear. How close is he to the
grunts? He starts out smelling the awful breath they get from
doing speed for night patrols.

> Going out at night the medics gave you pills,
> Dexedrine breath like dead snakes too long in a jar.
> I never saw the need for them myself, a little contact
> or anything that even sounded like contact would
> give me more speed than I could bear. . . . A couple
> rounds fired off in the dark a kilometer away and
> the Elephant would be there kneeling on my chest,
> sending me down into my boots for breath.

And from there, he shows the other side of the horror show
of war—a guy who's great at it—a long-range reconnaissance
patroller, "Lurp," in a tiger suit, with Dexedrine in one pocket
and downers in the other.

> I think he slept with his eyes open, and I was afraid
> of him anyway. All I ever managed was one quick

look in, and that was like looking at the floor of an ocean. He wore a gold earring and a headband torn from a piece of camouflage parachute material, and since nobody was about to tell him to get his hair cut it fell below his shoulders, covering a thick purple scar. Even at division he never went anywhere without at least a .45 and a knife, and he thought I was a freak because I wouldn't carry a weapon. . . . His face was all painted up for night walking like a bad hallucination, not like the painted faces I'd seen in San Francisco only a few weeks before, the other extreme of the same theater.

All these different people are like places on that earlier map. They're brought together by the accident of history and geography, but what unifies them is that they all pass through Herr's curious, loving, horrified, beautifully worried mind.

So right off, he readies us for voices weaving together and for radical shifts in tone from light to dark. As a writer you can't just start jamming stuff together, hoping the reader will magically know what's in your mind. You have to start out slowly, by laying transitions—like leaving breadcrumbs for the reader. Then the transitions get quicker through the book. As you get used to the method, the breadcrumbs grow fewer and eventually vanish. By the end, it's all sped-up jump cuts with invisible connections the reader's already mastered.

A serious student of memoir can pick apart or analyze any master this way to start dismantling the underlying architecture of an otherwise seamless piece of prose.

24 | Against Vanity: In Praise of Revision

The difference between the right word and the almost right word is the difference between lightning and a lightning bug.

Mark Twain

Every writer I know who's worth a damn spends way more time "losing" than "winning"—if success means typing a polished page that lands in print as is. Scriveners tend to arrive at good work through revision. Look at Yeats's chopped-up fixes in facsimile form, or Ezra Pound's swashbuckling edits of Eliot's *Waste Land*. Without radical overhaul, those works might have sunk like stones.

In fact, after a lifetime of hounding authors for advice, I've heard three truths from every mouth: (1) Writing is painful—it's "fun" only for novices, the very young, and hacks; (2) other than a few instances of luck, good work *only* comes through revision; (3) the best revisers often have reading habits that stretch back before the current age, which lends them a sense of history and raises their standards for quality.

Reading stuff in an antique-sounding idiom is hard for

many readers. Young, I hated the oldsters and often swallowed them with my nose pinched, as for a stank spoonful of cod-liver oil. They were rich and white and male. So I started off very slowly, reading closest to my time period and feeling my way back. Frank Conroy mentioned Robert Graves, who was just one generation back; Graves mentioned Samuel Johnson, whose biography I read first. T. S. Eliot mentioned Mallarmé and Valéry and Baudelaire. I started with existing heroes and read back through time.

Since I was always interested in how to be a writer, I also gobbled up literary biographies—Walter Jackson Bate on Keats and Coleridge; Enid Starkie on Baudelaire and Rimbaud; Diane Middlebrook on Anne Sexton; Ian Hamilton on Robert Lowell; Paul Mariani on William Carlos Williams. Getting a sense of the person's time in history often helped me to understand their styles in that context—what literary pressures and fashions and values of the day were forging their pages.

Reading through history cultivates in a writer a standard of quality higher than the marketplace. You can be a slave to current magazines or a slave to history. History's harder, but also more stable—and the books are better because they've been culled over time. Yes, the canon remains deeply flawed and has only begun to open up, but it's invariably true that work that's lasted for centuries has been sifted through over that time. Compare this to current work written to express a current trend or fashion—writing about 9/11, say. Writing to try to endure forever also lifts your eyes from the fickle vicis-situdes of the wickedly unfair (and often way-dumber-than-you-are) marketplace, which is populated by loads of frauds and charlatans.

Before you can work consciously, though, you go through a phase of developing a critical self, which makes a writer wicked self-conscious. Some students in our three-year MFA program come in defending every word; by mid-term second year, the more determined ones find themselves in despair at their own pages. Through reading and thinking, they've raised their taste beyond their skill levels. So when they stare down at their pages, they can no longer superimpose what's in their heads onto the work.

These students can't go back to their old tricks—they can see through those now. But the self-consciousness that hits them weighs them down. It's like trying to dance with armor strapped on, bulky and awkward. By third year, though, most seem to grow muscles to maneuver in that armor. The self-consciousness becomes simple awareness. Others can't stand to revise; instead they decide they're avant-garde, so everybody who doesn't like their work is unenlightened. (Note: being avant-garde is now . . . well, garde.)

Revision is the secret to their troubles—and yours. That, and a sense of quality that exceeds what you can do—that gives you something to strive for. Actually, every writer needs two selves—the generative self and the editor self.

In the early draft, the generative self shakes pom-poms at every pen stroke and cheers every crossed *t*. In a month or so, this diligent and optimistic creature gins out, say, two hundred pages.

The editor self then shows up to heft the pages, give a sniff, and say: *Yeah, but* . . . The editor condenses two hundred pages down to about thirty. I don't mean she cuts the rest; she may well boil the whole thing down so the same amount of stuff happens more economically.

The editor self thinks only of saving the reader time and shaping a powerful emotional experience. She can't turn her complaints and suspicions and doubts off.

I find generative me harder to get going. But through sheer hardheadedness, even I can grant myself permission to run buck-wild down the page with sentences dumb as stumps and few glimpses of anything pretty. The idea is to get some scenes down. Let your mind roam down some alleys that may land in dead ends—that's the nature of the process.

For *Lit*, I spent maybe two years writing about short stints in California and Mexico and the UK and some old boyfriends before I realized that those stories—by then hundreds of pages—lacked emotional gravitas. They were youthful years of drinking and frittering time away—shallow, easy, sparkly, rather than the more tormented phases in my life, which were less glisteny on the surface and, ergo, harder to rout out. Plus they had zip to do with my mother, whom I'd vowed not to write about anymore. But—surprise!—that was exactly what I needed to write about—how making peace with her legacy was something I had to do to become a mother myself.

Still, those early pages I threw away were somehow necessary, even if I wrote past them. They were way stations I needed to visit to eliminate them from the final itinerary.

In the beginning, when there are zero pages, you have to cheer yourself into cranking stuff out, even if it later lands on the cutting room floor. Each page takes you somewhere you need to travel before you can land in the next spot. You zigzag, and in the low moments, you just have to keep plodding on—saying the next small thing about which you feel strongly, trying to nestle down into that single instant of clear memory you know without shadow of doubt is both true and important to who you've become.

When it works, it's like a spell has been cast. For me, it's less the old world that comes in clear as the old me—how I felt, what I schemed about, who I lied to. But the writing's seldom pretty—the sentences are just banal.

The pushing comes when editor me comes back to comb over—and over and over—the pages, unpacking each moment. Mostly I take general ideas and try to show them carnally or in a dramatic story. I also interrogate a lot of what I believe: Are you sure that happened? How would he have told it differently? And because the carnal is where I write from, I write a lot of kinesthetic descriptions of my body in old spaces.

All the while, I question. Is this really crucial? Are you writing this part to pose as cool or smart?

For me, the last 20 percent of a book's improvement takes 95 percent of the effort—all in the editing. I can honestly say not one page I've ever published appears anywhere close to how it came out in first draft. A poem might take sixty versions. I am not much of a writer, but I am a stubborn little bulldog of a reviser.

In the long run, the revision process feels better if you approach it with curiosity. Each editorial mark can't register as a "mistake" that threatens the spider ego. Remind yourself that revising proves your care for the reader and of the nature of your ambition. Writing, regardless of the end result—whether good or bad, published or not, well reviewed or slammed—means celebrating beauty in an often ugly world. And you do that by fighting for elegance and beauty, redoing or cutting the flabby, disordered parts.

There's a strange freedom in keeping the bar so high that—poor me—I'll never make it over. If Shakespeare's my standard, I'm at least free from worrying about the muddy, fickle sales market. Oddly, when I'm working well, the work ceases being about me, even in memoir.

Rewriting on the page is safer than revision in, say, painting, where you can paint past a good place and wreck a canvas. Performers can't revise at all. A writer can always go back to an earlier draft. The point is to have more curiosity about possible forms the work could take than sense of self-protection for your ego.

So try learning how to cut out the dull parts. Even the smallest towns have coffee shop bulletin boards or community centers with a writer's workshop now. Even the less good groups can help you by speaking for your potential reader—they're way better than the echo chamber of your own head.

One of the greatest memoirs of all time is G. H. Hardy's *A Mathematician's Apology*. Nearing the end of his life, Hardy felt his mathematical abilities wane and tried to kill himself. He was a nerdy guy with few deep emotional connections, a Sunday cricket-watching bachelor of the type the UK breeds. His friend from Cambridge, C. P. Snow, found him in the hospital, bleakly mocking what a mess he'd made of his near-fatal overdose. Snow's intro to Hardy's story is heart-rending:

> As a touch of farce, he had a black eye. Vomiting from the drugs, he had hit his head on the lavatory basin. . . . I had to enter into the sarcastic game. I had never felt less like sarcasm, but I had to play. I talked about

other distinguished failures at bringing it off. What about the German generals in the last war?

Hardy decided to go on living. Snow says, "His hard, intellectual stoicism came back." But he was infirm, and he waited for death as many of the infirm elderly do. As most of us someday will.

Hardy's survival is a profound act of courage, and often when I've been despondent about my own work, or when that ghoul, self-pity, has tempted me from the shadows—*Your work is aggressively minor, you poser!*—I've taken comfort in Hardy's slender book about a subject that bored me until his passion became contagious.

Hardy ends with one of the most brutal, yet somehow hopeful, credos for anybody trying to make anything.

> I have never done anything "useful." No discovery
> of mine has made or is likely to make, directly or
> indirectly, for good or ill, the least difference to the
> amenity of the world. . . . Judged by all practical
> standards, the value of my mathematical life is nil,
> and outside mathematics it is trivial anyhow. . . .
> I have added something to knowledge and helped
> others to add more; and these somethings have a value
> that differs in degree only, and not in kind, from that
> of the creations of the great mathematicians, or any of
> the other artists, great or small, who have left some
> kind of memorial behind them.

I often hand this out to students as they graduate, to remind them that anybody struggling to make something—no matter how they succeed or don't in terms of the marketplace—has entered into conversation with giants. We're all in the same arena, and our efforts differ "in degree only, and not in kind."

Just picking up a pen makes you part of a tradition of writers that dates thousands of years back and includes Homer and Toni Morrison and cave artists sketching buffalo. It's a corny attitude to revere writers in this celebrity age, when even academics cry the author is dead. Go to any book award ceremony, and we're like America's Homeliest Video. We are the inward-looking goofballs who spill on our blouses and look befuddled in our selfies.

But I still feel awe for us—yes, for the masters who wrought lasting beauty from their hard lives, but for the rest of us, too, for the great courage all of us show in trying to wring some truth from the godawful mess of a single life. To bring oneself to others makes the whole planet less lonely. The nobility of everybody trying boggles the mind.

And I'd like to leave you thinking about diffident old Hardy, who—by his own yardstick—failed. He did no work as lastingly beautiful and relevant as, say, Einstein or Newton. I'm no judge of his mathematical work, which may or may not be as minor as he finds it, yet this book he thought so little of, still published by a small press, is the most widely read memoir by a mathematician I know. And every time I read it, it showers me with sparkles like a Disney fairy. None of us can ever know the value of our lives, or how our separate and silent scribbling may add to the amenity of the world, if only by how radically it changes us, one and by one.

Acknowledgments

Wild gratitude to agent extraordinaire, Amanda Urban; Harper-Collins publisher, Jonathan Burnham; and my incomparable editrix, Jennifer Barth, who steered me out of so many fogs. Final readers Mark Costello, Larissa MacFarquhar, and Geoffrey Wolff also kept me rowing when I was weary. All honor to your names.

Appendix | Required Reading— Mostly Memoirs and Some Hybrids

The asterisked memoirs are books I've taught. Does this mean they're better written? Absolutely.

*Adams, Henry. *The Education of Henry Adams* and *Mont-Saint-Michel and Chartres*.

*Allende, Isabel. *The Sum of Our Days*.

*Als, Hilton. *The Women*.

Amis, Martin. *Experience*.

*Angelou, Maya. *I Know Why the Caged Bird Sings*.

Antrim, Donald. *The Afterlife*.

*Arenas, Reinaldo. *Before Night Falls*.

Ayer, Pico. *Falling Off the Map*.

*Saint Augustine. *Confessions*.

Baldwin, James. *Notes of a Native Son*.

*Batuman, Elif. *The Possessed: Adventures with Russian Books and the People Who Read Them*.

*Beah, Ishmael. *A Long Way Gone*.

Beck, Edward. *God Underneath: Spiritual Memoirs of a Catholic Priest*.

*Bernhard, Thomas. *Gathering Evidence*.

*Black Elk. *Black Elk Speaks*.

Blow, Charles M. *Fire Shut Up in My Bones*.

Bourdain, Anthony. *Kitchen Confidential*.

Boyett, Micha. *Found: A Story of Questions, Grace, and Everyday Prayer*.

Brave Bird, Mary. *Lakota Woman*.

Brickhouse, Jamie. *Dangerous When Wet*.

*Brown, Claude. *Manchild in the Promised Land*.

*Buford, Bill. *Among the Thugs* and *Heat*.

Burgess, Anthony. *Little Wilson and Big God: Being the First Part of the Confessions of Anthony Burgess.*

Busch, Benjamin. *Dust to Dust.*

Cairns, Scott. *Short Trip to the Edge.*

Carr, David. *The Night of the Gun.*

Carroll, James. *Practicing Catholic.*

*Chaudhuri, Nirad C. *The Autobiography of an Unknown Indian.*

*Chatwin, Bruce. *In Patagonia.*

Chast, Roz. *Can't We Talk About Something More Pleasant?*

*Cheever, Susan. *Home Before Dark.*

*Cherry-Garrard, Apsley. *The Worst Journey in the World.*

Churchill, Winston. *My Early Life, 1874–1904.*

Ciszek, Walter, SJ. *With God in Russia.*

*Coetzee, J. M. *Boyhood.*

Collins, Judy. *Singing Lessons: A Memoir of Love, Loss, Hope, and Healing.*

*Conroy, Frank. *Stop-Time.*

Conway, Jill Ker. *The Road from Coorain.*

Covington, Dennis. *Salvation on Sand Mountain.*

*Crews, Harry. *A Childhood: The Biography of a Place* and *Blood and Grits.*

*Crick, Francis, and James Watson. *The Double Helix.*

Crowell, Rodney. *Chinaberry Sidewalks.*

Dau, John Bul. *God Grew Tired of Us.*

*Day, Dorothy. *The Long Loneliness.*

*Dinesen, Isak. *Out of Africa.*

*Didion, Joan. *The Year of Magical Thinking.*

*Dillard, Annie. *An American Childhood.*

*Doty, Mark. *Heaven's Coast.*

Douglass, Frederick. *Narrative of the Life of Frederick Douglass, an American Slave.*

*Du Bois, W. E. B. *The Souls of Black Folk.*

Dubus, Andre, III. *Townie.*

Dunham, Lena. *Not That Kind of Girl.*

Dylan, Bob. *Chronicles.*

Eggers, Dave. *A Heartbreaking Work of Staggering Genius.*

Eire, Carlos. *Waiting for Snow in Havana: Confessions of a Cuban Boy.*

*Exley, Frederick. *A Fan's Notes.*

Fey, Tina. *Bossypants.*

Forna, Aminatta. *The Devil That Danced on the Water.*

Fox, Paula. *Borrowed Finery.*

Frame, Janet. *An Autobiography.*

Frankl, Viktor. *Man's Search for Meaning.*

Franklin, Benjamin. *The Autobiography of Benjamin Franklin.*

*Frazier, Ian. *On the Rez.*

Frenkel, Edward. *Love and Math.*

Fuller, Alexandra. *Don't Let's Go to the Dogs Tonight.*

*García Márquez, Gabriel. *Living to Tell the Tale.*

Gellhorn, Martha. *Travels With Myself and Another.*

Geronimo. *My Life.*

Gilbert, Elizabeth. *Eat, Pray, Love.*

*Ginzburg, Yevgenia. *Journey into the Whirlwind.*

*Gourevitch, Philip. *We Wish to Inform You that Tomorrow We Will Be Killed with Our Families.*

*Graves, Robert. *Good-Bye to All That.*

Gray, Francine du Plessix. *Them: A Memoir of Parents.*

Grealy, Lucy. *Autobiography of a Face.*

Greene, Graham. *A Sort of Life.*

Guevara, Ernesto Che. *The Motorcycle Diaries.*

*Haley, Alex, and Malcolm X. *The Autobiography of Malcolm X.*

Hamilton, Gabrielle. *Blood, Bones & Butter.*

Hampl, Patricia. *A Romantic Education.*

*Hardy, G. H. *A Mathematician's Apology.*

*Harrison, Kathryn. *The Kiss.*

*Haxton, Brooks. *Fading Hearts on the River: A Life in High-Stakes Poker.*

*Hemingway, Ernest. *A Moveable Feast.*

*Herr, Michael. *Dispatches.*

*Hickey, Dave. *Air Guitar.*

Hogan, Linda. *The Woman Who Watches Over the World.*

Hongo, Garrett. *Volcano: A Memoir of Hawai'i.*

Hooks, Bell. *Bone Black.*

Huang, Eddie. *Fresh Off the Boat.*

*Hurston, Zora Neale. *Dust Tracks on a Road.*

Irving, Debby. *Waking Up White.*

Jackson, Phil. *Sacred Hoops.*

Jacobs, Harriet. *Incidents in the Life of a Slave Girl.*

Jamison, Kay. *An Unquiet Mind.*

Jordan, June. *Soldier: A Poet's Childhood.*
Keller, Helen. *The Story of My Life.*
Kidder, Tracy. *House.*
*Kincaid, Jamaica. *My Brother.*
King, Stephen. *On Writing.*
*Kingston, Maxine Hong. *The Woman Warrior.*
Knausgård, Karl Ove. The *Min Kamp* (*My Struggle*) series.
*Krakauer, Jon. *Into Thin Air.*
Lawrence, T. E. *Seven Pillars of Wisdom.*
Least Heat-Moon, William. *Blue Highways: A Journey into America.*
*Levi, Primo. *Survival in Auschwitz.*
*Lewis, C. S. *Surprised by Joy.*
Liao Yiwu. *For a Song and a Hundred Songs: A Poet's Journey
    Through a Chinese Prison.*
Lopate, Philip. *Against Joie de Vivre.*
*Lorde, Audre. *Zami: A New Spelling of My Name.*
*Lowell, Robert. "91 Revere Street," in *Life Studies.*
Macdonald, Helen. *H Is for Hawk.*
Malan, Rian. *My Traitor's Heart.*
Mandela, Nelson. *Conversations with Myself.*
*Mandelstam, Nadezhda. *Hope Against Hope* and *Hope Abandoned.*
Manguso, Sarah. *The Two Kinds of Decay.*
*Mantel, Hilary. *Giving Up the Ghost.*
*Markham, Beryl. *West with the Night.*
Martin, Steve. *Born Standing Up.*
*Matthiessen, Peter. *The Snow Leopard.*
Mayle, Peter. *A Year in Provence.*
*McBride, James. *The Color of Water.*
McCarthy, Mary. *Memories of a Catholic Girlhood.*
*McCourt, Frank. *Angela's Ashes.*
McPhee, John. *Coming into the Country.*
*Merton, Thomas. *The Seven Storey Mountain.*
*Milburn, Michael. *Odd Man In.*
*Mingus, Charles. *Beneath the Underdog.*
Momaday, N. Scott. *The Names.*
Monette, Paul. *Borrowed Time: An AIDS Memoir.*
Moody, Anne. *Coming of Age in Mississippi.*
Murakami, Haruki. *What I Talk About When I Talk About Running.*

*Nabokov, Vladimir. *Speak, Memory.*
Nafisi, Azar. *Reading Lolita in Tehran: A Memoir in Books.*
*Neruda, Pablo. *Memoirs.*
Nolan, Ty. *Memoir of a Reluctant Shaman.*
Norris, Kathleen. *The Cloister Walk.*
Oates, Joyce Carol. *A Widow's Story.*
Olsen, Tillie. *Silences.*
*Ondaatje, Michael. *Running in the Family.*
O'Rourke, Meghan. *The Long Goodbye.*
Orwell, George. *Homage to Catalonia, Burmese Days*, and
    Down and Out in Paris and London.
Parker, Mary Louise. *Dear Mr. You.*
*Patchett, Ann. *Truth & Beauty.*
Pirsig, Robert. *Zen and the Art of Motorcycle Maintenance.*
Raban, Jonathan. *Bad Land.*
Radziwill, Carole. *What Remains.*
Raphael, Lev. *My Germany.*
Red Cloud, with Bob Drury and Tom Clavin.
    The Heart of Everything That Is.
Reed, Ishmael. *Blues City.*
Rios, Albert. *Capirotada: A Nogales Memoir.*
*Rodriguez, Richard. *Hunger of Memory:*
    The Education of Richard Rodriguez.
Roth, Marco. *The Scientists.*
Russell, Bertrand. *The Autobiography of Bertrand Russell.*
*St Aubyn, Edward. The Patrick Melrose novels.
Sallans, Ryan. *Second Son.*
Santiago, Esmeralda. *When I Was Puerto Rican.*
Sartre, Jean-Paul. *The Words.*
*Sassoon, Siegfried. *Memoirs of an Infantry Officer.*
*Shackleton, Ernest. *South: The Endurance Expedition.*
Shakur, Assata. *Assata.*
Shakur, Sanyika. *Monster: The Autobiography of an L.A. Gang Member.*
*Shteyngart, Gary. *Little Failure.*
Sleigh, Tom. *Interview with a Ghost.*
Smith, Patti. *Just Kids.*
Smith, Tracy K. *Ordinary Light.*
Solomon, Andrew. *The Noonday Demon.*

Sontag, Susan. *Illness as Metaphor.*
Soto, Jock. *Every Step You Take.*
Stahl, Jerry. *Permanent Midnight.*
Strayed, Cheryl. *Wild.*
Tan, Amy. *The Opposite of Fate: A Book of Musings.*
Theroux, Paul. *Old Patagonian Express.*
Tolstoy, Leo. *Childhood, Boyhood, Youth.*
Thompson, Ahmir-Khalib. *Mo' Meta Blues: The World According to Questlove.*
Thompson, Hunter S. *Fear and Loathing in Las Vegas.*
Trillin, Calvin. *About Alice.*
*Twain, Mark. *Autobiography of Mark Twain.*
Walls, Jeannette. *The Glass Castle.*
Wainaina, Binyavanga. *One Day I Will Write About This Place.*
Washington, Booker T. *Up from Slavery.*
Watt, Robert Lee. *The Black Horn.*
Weil, Simone. *Waiting for God, Gravity and Grace.*
*Welty, Eudora. *One Writer's Beginnings.*
White, Edmund. *My Lives.*
White, T.H. *The Goshawk.*
*Wideman, John Edgar. *Brothers and Keepers.*
*Wiesel, Elie. *Night.*
Winterson, Jeanette. *Why Be Happy When You Could Be Normal?*
*Wolfe, Tom. *The Electric Kool-Aid Acid Test.*
*Wolff, Geoffrey. *The Duke of Deception* and *A Day at the Beach.*
*Wolff, Tobias. *This Boy's Life* and *In Pharaoh's Army.*
Woolf, Virginia. *Moments of Being.*
*Wright, Richard. *American Hunger.*
*Yen Mah, Adeline. *Falling Leaves: The Memoir of an Unwanted Chinese Daughter.*
Zailckas, Koren. *Smashed: Story of a Drunken Girlhood.*

USEFUL BOOKS ABOUT MEMOIR
Adams, Timothy Dow. *Telling Lies in Modern American Autobiography.*
Leibowitz, Herbert. *Fabricating Lives.*
Shields, David. *Reality Hunger.*
Yagoda, Ben. *Memoir: A History.*

Permissions

About the Author

MARY KARR is the author of three award-winning, bestselling memoirs: *The Liars' Club*, *Cherry*, and *Lit*. A Guggenheim Fellow in poetry, Karr has won Pushcart Prizes for both verse and essays. Other grants include the Whiting Writer's Award, PEN's Martha Albrand Award, and Radcliffe's Bunting Fellowship. She is the Jesse Truesdell Peck Professor of Literature at Syracuse University.